A Story
A Folk Tale
and Other
Stories

A Saint, A Folk Tale and Other Stories

Lesser-Known Monuments of India

RANA SAFVI

RUPA

Published by
Rupa Publications India Pvt. Ltd 2021
7/16, Ansari Road, Daryaganj
New Delhi 110002

Sales centres:
Prayagraj Bengaluru Chennai
Hyderabad Jaipur Kathmandu
Kolkata Mumbai

ISBN: 978-93-5520-085-3

Fourth impression 2023

10 9 8 7 6 5 4

Dedicated to the artisans who gave their lives to leaving behind monuments for posterity.

Meri mahbub unhen bhi to mohabbat hogi
Jin ki sannai ne bakhshi hai use shakl-e-jamil
Un ke pyaron ke maqabir rahe benam-o-numud
Aaj tak un pe jalai na kisi ne qindil

—Sahir Ludhianvi

My love, they must have also loved
They, whose artistry bestowed it this beautiful shape
The tombs of their loved ones, remain forgotten
Till now no one has even lit a candle to their memory

'Without architecture, we cannot remember...'
—John Ruskin, *The Seven Lamps of Architecture*

Contents

Preface

Architecture has always fascinated me and over the years, I have visited innumerable monuments in India and abroad. I often say that my spirit roams abandoned places, listening to their story and trying to hear their tale.

That is why, perhaps, I chose to tell the tale of monuments rather than people.

India, with its ancient civilization and all its diversity, is a paradise for someone who loves heritage like I do. These past five to six years, I have been travelling extensively in India but I have still not managed to visit more than a small percentage of the glorious built heritage that we have.

I have always had a penchant for travelling off the beaten path and a fascination for the unknown. So whenever I visited a city, town or village, I would hire a local autorickshaw, taxi or at times even a cycle rickshaw and tell them to take me to all the oldest parts of their city. Sometimes I came across such gems, that the sight is enough to wipe off the tiredness of sore muscles and aching legs. Whichever place I visit I take innumerable photographs and videos, in which I describe everything, and these serve as my notes. I also interview locals to get their opinion and document oral history.

I have had many adventures along the way, met some extremely interesting people and kind strangers, enjoyed local hospitality and food, fallen sick, had fun times and in a nutshell, lived life to its fullest.

In one city, I only had a day so I spent 10 hours exploring and visited a bounty of heritage places. The heart app on my iPhone showed 18,455 steps that day and my feet wanted to give up on me, but I work with the philosophy of 'After all, tomorrow is another day!' This book is a result of some of my travels and impressions. It is in no way a comprehensive description of the monuments or a list of monuments that a person should visit, but I hope it serves as a suggestion. I hope it sets off the readers on a discovery of their own.

Before We Explore

Indian architecture offers one of the most glorious forms of built heritage anywhere in the world. Before we start exploring, a small note on the nature of the buildings I have covered.

India, with its geographical expanse, rich history and diversity, offers a veritable feast for the senses in every way, especially its spectacular range of built heritage.

Starting from the earliest cave-shelter paintings, rock-cut architecture, the first urban cities of the Indus Valley Civilization to modern skyscrapers, India has it all.

Ancient Indian architects and artisans graduated from rock-cut architecture to carving structural forms from mountain mass as in the famous Kailasha Temple in Ellora, Aurangabad.

From rock-cut architecture to elaborately carved and sculpted temples with trabeate style (column and beam), to grand tombs and mosques in the arcuate (column and arch), India has it all.

The four main dimensions of large masonry buildings in structural terms were walls, columns, beams and arches.

What distinguished one architectural form or style from another was the manner in which these dimensions were combined with the materials of construction and type of decoration. From this point of view, the specific features of buildings erected by immigrant Muslims in India were arches, domes, minarets, mihrab, geometrical and floral patterns, and calligraphy in the Arabic script on stone, all of which were quite distinct from such elements in pre-Muslim India.[1]

The arrival of the Turks in the twelfth century saw many architectural designs and techniques being incorporated in existing building techniques which gave rise to the unique architecture which is called 'Indo-Islamic'. This term is now contested but frequently used as it differentiates it from similar architecture in the Islamicate world.

ROCK-CUT ARCHITECTURE

The earliest man lived in caves or rock shelters and it was thus natural that they built their places of worship in them. In the Indian context, rock-cut architecture is a glorious reminder and specimen of the skill, enterprise, endeavour and piety of Indians through the ages. These were closely associated with various religions and religious activities.

If Bhimbetka caves in Madhya Pradesh (MP) are one of the earliest remains of rock shelters, with their paintings spanning the prehistoric Palaeolithic and Mesolithic period, then it's the Barabar Caves from third century in Bihar, which are the first rock-cut caves that we have. The latter is no surprise, for Buddhism and Jainism flowered and flourished here. We find more in Maharashtra in the next stage.

A Saint, a Folk Tale and Other Stories

The first ruler under whom rock-cut architecture developed was Ashoka, who had turned to Buddhism and made it his life's mission to propagate the teachings of Lord Buddha and commemorate his relics.

The rock-cut caves were excavated from the rocks by the Buddhist monks for prayer and residence purposes as *chaityas* (prayer halls) or *viharas* (monasteries) or stupas. Taking inspiration from wooden structures, they carved windows, balconies, doorways and ogee-shaped arches into the rocks. In that sense, we could also call them sculpted from the rocks.

Rock-cut architecture occupies a very important place in the history of Indian architecture.

TEMPLE

Ancient Indian temples are classified into two broad types: the Nagara or the northern style and the Dravida or the southern style. The mixed style was known as the Vesara style. This emerged during the Gupta era (fourth–seventh century CE).

The basic prototype of a Nagara temple emerged in the Gupta period with its large plinth, pillared main hall (mandap), inner sanctum (garbha griha) topped by a *shikhara* (spire or pyramidal roof) and a gallery for circumambulation. In the earlier temples, the mandap would be away from the sanctum but later they were united by a vestibule or *antaral.* A large temple had many mandapas and few had transepts (wings on either side) or maha-mandapa.

Later it culminated in each part being distinct with its own shikharas graded according to their position, with the lowest being on the porch and the tallest one on the inner sanctum. The surface would be profusely decorated with carvings of gods, goddesses, kings and scenes from everyday life of ordinary people.

A large *gopuram* (a monumental tower), usually ornate, at the entrance of the temple was the main feature of the Dravida style. The top of the temple in this style is usually in the shape of a rectangular-truncated pyramid.

The Aihole group of temples in Karnataka mark the shift from rock-cut temples to stone blocks for vertical construction. While the cave temples had a simple cella in a verandah-like construction, now the temples had a garbha griha, a mandapa (sanctum) and enclosed sabha mandapa (assembly hall), an antechamber and a *pradakshina pratha* (circumambulation path). The Aihole temples have flat or sloping roofs, which resemble thatched cottages. Some of the temples do have a small upper storey or shikhara on these sloping roofs which are probably later additions to the structure.

Pattadakkal in Karnataka is the only site which has temples of Nagara and Dravida style present next to each other. Aihole offers an example of the Vesara style.

MOSQUES

A Muslim is supposed to pray five times a day at the prescribed timings. These prayers can be conducted in any place which is clean and legitimately owned (if not one's own then permission has to be taken from the owner). Great emphasis is placed on congregational prayers to increase the feeling of brotherhood as the latter is greatly encouraged in Islam.

The word for mosque in Arabic is masjid which comes from *sujood/sajda* or prostration. Thus, a masjid is a place of prostration. One can have a place of prostration on a prayer rug at home or spread out in the wilderness but the term is usually applied to a religious building where people can pray as a congregation.

The first mosque in Islam is the Quba Mosque in Medina, built in the lifetime of the Prophet Muhammad, who is said to have placed the first stones for it. I am fortunate to have visited it and prayed there.

The essential feature of a mosque is a Qibla (the word qibla literally means direction) wall or a wall which indicates the direction of Qibla (Mecca). It is enjoined on Muslims to pray facing Mecca. These are usually in the shape of niche arches set in the wall which may be very elaborately ornamented or simple.

Apart from this, one can have a *mimbar* or pulpit near the qibla mihrab for the Imam (religious leader) to read sermons from and a *hauz* for ablutions which are essential before praying. There are set rules prescribed for this. The tank should be of a certain size and depth, if not, it should have flowing water.

Not every mosque is a Jama Masjid. The Jama Masjid is the mosque where the Friday sermon and Friday prayers are read.

TOMBS AND MAUSOLEUMS

In Islam, burial should ideally be done within 24 hours and these are preceded by a few funerary rituals. The first of these is the ceremonial bath (ghusl) followed by the shrouding of the body in a simple white cloth (kafan) and then the funeral prayers. The body is buried only in this simple shroud without any coffin. The burial can take place immediately after the shrouding or be delayed so that relatives and loved ones can pay respect.

The grave is perpendicular to the direction of the Qibla so that the body, placed in the grave lying on its right side, faces the Qibla. As per Sharia laws, the grave should be simple with or without a marker, which should also be very simple. The body of the deceased is merged with the soil and it is the soul which is left. The grave is thus an abode of the soul and not the body. The grave is just the first stage of the journey of the soul into the hereafter and the decision on Judgment Day, whether it enters heaven or hell.

Since a simple mud grave is all that is permissible as per Sharia, those who wanted to build memorials made a cenotaph on top with a building erected around it while the underground chamber would house the unmarked mud grave. The cenotaph is just a replica and not the actual grave and could thus be carved or elaborately ornamented.

As the soul needs prayers for an easy journey into the hereafter, mosques were built next to it for prayers and recitation of the Quran, which could be consecrated for deliverance of the dead person's soul.

These tombs and mosques could be as elaborate as the Taj Mahal or as simple as Princess Jahanara Begum's grave in the dargah of Hazrat Nizamuddin Auliya.

MAZAAR AND DARGAH

The burial place of a saint is called a *mazaar* or *dargah* and is called shrine in English. Mazaar is an Arabic word that

A Saint, a Folk Tale and Other Stories

comes from the word *ziyarat* or pious visitation/pilgrimage. Dargah is derived from a Persian word which literally means threshold or entrance and is reserved for shrines built over the grave/relics of an important saint.

Visits to mazaars and dargahs are to ask for the saints to intercede on behalf of the visitor with God, whereas one visits graves to pray for the deceased person's soul.

Today, tombs and mausoleums have become tourist attractions and their original purpose of providing spiritual succour for the deceased one's soul has long been forgotten. I try and make it a point to recite Surah Fatiha whenever I visit a graveyard, tomb or mausoleum.

In India, Sufi saints are credited with unusual powers and it is believed by their devotees that they can communicate people's wishes to God, for even after the death, his inspirational power (baraka) received from God is sent out. Thus, visitors flock to his shrine to ask for intercession for their desires.

IMAMBARA

An imambara/imambargah means the house of the Imam.

It is the place where congregational assemblies called *majlis* are held to commemorate the sacrifices of Imam Husain, the grandson of Prophet Muhammad who was martyred along with friends and male members of his family in the Battle of Karbala by Yazid, the ruler of Syria.

Though most imambaras have an attached masjid, they are not the same as mosques. Of course one can offer their prayers inside it, but there will not be regular congregational prayer in it.

The imambaras are built south facing and the western wall of the hall can be used for namaz.

The imambara, like a mosque, can be small or elaborate.

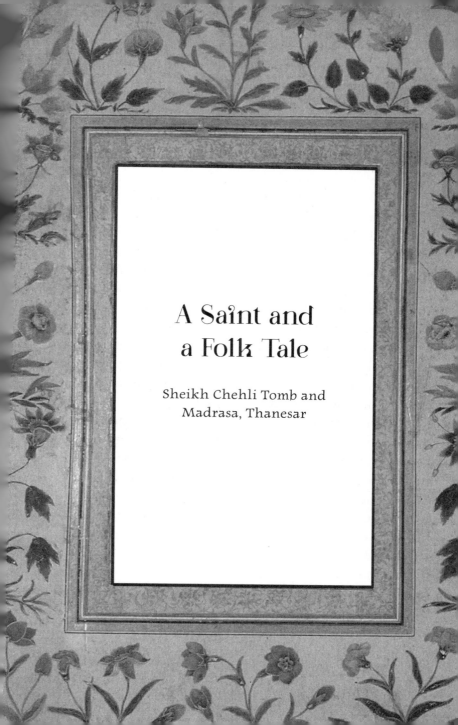

A Saint and
a Folk Tale

Sheikh Chehli Tomb and
Madrasa, Thanesar

Our favourite bedtime stories as children used to be about a simpleton called Sheikh Chilli, whose life was a never-ending saga of goof-ups resulting in hilarious anecdotes. Of course, as children we thought that these were fictitious and no such character existed. It is only now that I realize these tales were to teach moral values to children about the hollowness of the world and the perils of attaching too much importance to material things, using either a composite character or an actual person.

Sheikh Chilli was always thrown into situations where he tried to follow a simple piece of learning from his elders (usually mother) but was sidetracked by outside influences to adapt which led to weird situations, ultimately leading to the lesson that it is better to follow one's own conscience and the path shown by older and wiser people.

A story in point is when he was once told by his mother to always believe in simple living, high thinking and speaking sweetly to all. He understands that as '*ooncha baitho, meetha bolo* (sit on something high and speak sweetly)'.

So, when he goes to his in-law's house he refuses to sit on a chair and climbs atop the tallest piece of furniture in the room, which was an almirah. When he is offered food, he refuses to eat anything except gulab jamun because how else will he speak sweetly?

This leads to further hilarious situations where everyone has their own suggestions to give, and poor Sheikh Chilli tries to follow them.

His mother-in-law then explains what the advice given to him by his mother actually meant. We would be in splits imagining a man sitting on an almirah devouring gulab jamuns but would eventually learn something from it.

These stories would then end in an explanation given to us by our elders on the virtues of humanity, living a good life and doing good to others.

These stories were presented in such a way that children connected to them and at the same time had a laugh as well.

So, I was extremely surprised to find that there was a tomb of a Sufi saint named Sheikh Chilli in Thanesar and that he was in fact supposed to be Dara Shukoh's spiritual master. Dara Shukoh, the mystic prince and eldest son of Shah Jahan, is known for his scholarly attainments; no master of his could have been a simpleton! He may have been simple as all Sufis lived ascetic lives and were renowned for their humility, but he would definitely have been very wise. Thus started my quest to find out about our childhood's favourite character and his connection to an ill-fated prince. The result was quite surprising.

The first sign that he was not the simpleton of my childhood came from signposts in Thanesar that gave directions to a Sheikh Chehli's tomb. The word Chehli means 40 and that was my first clue that it could possibly be a saint who had done a *chillah* or a 40-day solitary, spiritual retreat and the word Chilli could have been a corruption of that.

Sufi saints were famous for doing chillahs, influenced by the yogic practices of India. There are many *chillahgahs* associated with the famous Sufi saint Baba Farid in Delhi and Punjab.

The signboards leading to it were very good and as we approached it, I was taken aback by the sheer size of the complex. A huge enclosing wall, with cupolas and pavilions surrounds it. A tall gateway in the eastern wall leads inside the complex and up to a courtyard with a lovely tank in the middle of a well-maintained garden and galleries with rooms on all four sides. The Archaeological Survey of India (ASI) has now turned two of these galleries into museums for visitors. The grounds and the museum are beautifully maintained and obviously very popular with the locals for even on a hot summer weekday it was quite packed with visitors.

The tomb itself is accessible through staircases in the north galleries and built on a high platform is really majestic. But what were these galleries for? Research led me to Subhash Parihar's book, *Some Aspects of Indo-Islamic Architecture*. He describes it as a madrasa and one of the three built by the Mughals. A madrasa literally means a place for study and according to Parihar these three were probably meant for educating the *ulema* for civil and judicial service in the empire. Two of them are in Delhi, namely the Khairul Manazil opposite Purana Qila and Ghaziuddin Khan ka Madrasa, now Anglo Arabic College, near Ajmeri gate. The third was in Thanesar as this city was on the Grand Trunk Road.

I walked up the stairs onto a large platform with a very low octagonal marble base that had a perforated design and marble rail running around it, on which stands the lovely octagonal marble tomb, overlooking the madrasa. I could see with exquisite screens for air and light on all sides of it. The tomb door was closed so I could only peep in to see the two cenotaphs inside. The actual graves are, of course, underground in a lower chamber. The lower chamber is connected to the madrasa through a narrow gallery.

The tomb is built of buff sandstone and is crowned with a white pear-shaped, marble dome standing on a high circular drum, topped with a sturdy finial. The combination of white and buff is very soothing. The upper octagonal chamber has an eave and the base of the drum is trimmed with a delicate, ornamented, white railing.

Another tomb with a vaulted roof on the western wall was open so I went inside. This was said to be the saint's wife.

The very obvious Persian influence in the architecture as well as use of marble invariably brings up comparison to the Taj Mahal, but to my eye there seemed to be none.

The madrasa is built around a courtyard with a central tank and has nine arched openings on each side. This is on the Charbagh plan of Persian architecture theme popular in that era.

The Charbagh was a paradisiacal theme with its flowing water channels and bodies symbolizing the four rivers of heaven. All this imagery is supposed to help the soul of the dead person gain forgiveness and gain entry into paradise.

Humayun's Tomb was the first tomb built on this Persian principle of Charbagh or paradisiacal tombs.

The outer walls of the complex have 12 cupolas with traces of glazed tiles showing.

The signs there give the name of the saint as Abd-ur-Rahim Abdul-Karim Abd-ur-Razak, but Parihar has an interesting take on it. The only important saint of Thanesar from Akbar's era, Sheikh Jalaluddin Thanesari, is built nearby so it obviously wasn't him. He writes that none of the leading saints of Thanesar fit the bill. Dara Shukoh's spiritual master was a Sufi saint of the Qadriya order, Mullah Shah Badakshi of Kashmir and not Sheikh Chehli. This legend can be attributed to a report by Sir Alexander Cunningham in 1862–65 where he identifies the tomb as belonging to the spiritual advisor of Dara Shukoh. Cunningham writes that his real name is in dispute and he is known in the area as Sheikh Chillie or Sheikh Tilli.

The madrasa itself is dated to mid-seventeenth century when Dara Shukoh was powerful in the Mughal court and seems to be his work as he encouraged intellectual pursuits. Fittingly, one of the rooms in the complex is a Dara Shukoh Library.

According to Parihar, this tomb was turned into a gurudwara by the Sikhs in the last century but the 'British rulers reinstated the tombstones in it. Later it was restored by the Archaeological Survey of India.'[2]

The tomb was in ruins and John Dawkins, the then collector of Thaneshar, was instrumental in getting the tomb repaired in AD 1854.

Thanesar was a well-known centre of the Sufi Chisti *silsilah* and according to Parihar it is possible that Dara Shukoh wanted to promote the Qadriya silsilah and built the madrasa for that purpose. The saint buried there must have been a teacher at the madrasa from the Qadriya silsilah and definitely wise to have headed it.

Chisti, Qadriya, Suhrawardi and Naqshbandi are the four main orders in the subcontinent. The Qadiriya silsilah was named after Sheikh Abdul Qadir Jilani, born in 1077–78 CE in the Irani town of Jilan. It is the oldest of all Sufi silsilahs though it came to India in the fourteenth century when the Chisti order was well established in the subcontinent.

Sheikh Jalaluddin Thanesari was from the Sabiri silsilah, an offshoot of the Chisti silsilah. His simple tomb attracts many visitors and during the time I was there, I saw devotees from far and wide gathered there.

The Pathar Masjid near the madrasa complex looked very interesting but it was locked so I could only admire its red sandstone architecture from afar. The Masjid appears to have been built in the seventeenth century CE.

The nearby Harsh ka Tila, with excavation sites, is an added bonus for visitors. This site, which extends over 1,750 kilometres was excavated by B.M. Pandey of the ASI and throws significant light on successive city settlement ranging from first century to nineteenth century CE.

Just as in the Sheikh Chilli story, a sense of calm and serenity pervades the complex, taking you back through the remains of monuments through the centuries. The simple lesson I learnt there was of impermanence of material things and the permanence of spiritual values and piety.

A Queen's Forgotten Resting Place

Aahukhana, Burhanpur

Having grown up in Uttar Pradesh (UP) and lived in Agra, the Taj Mahal was a familiar sight to me. I had visited it innumerable times but I had never spared a thought for Burhanpur where Mumtaz Mahal had died and had been initially buried. It was in search of her first burial place that I went to Burhanpur and as someone whose spirit is in tune with ruins, was rewarded with riches beyond compare.

The word *burhan* means demonstration or proof and true to its meaning, Burhanpur stands witness to the initial tears and sorrow of the grief-stricken husband and children of Mumtaz Mahal.

But let's take a tour of the city first.

Once a thriving Mughal city known as the 'Gateway to the Deccan', it is now a sleepy town, which to me looks stuck in a time warp. Unlike most other walled cities, the city walls of Burhanpur, MP are still intact, as are the gateways. I drove through the Shanwara Gate, Itwara Gate and Shikarpura Gate. Other gateways are named Lohar Mandi Gate, Dilli Gate, Sindhipura Gate, Silampura Gate and Rajpura Gate.

Beautiful wooden houses coexist with cement ones, though lack of heritage management is proving tough on the former. Tongas still ply as a regular means of transport.

The earliest rulers of the area were the Rashtrakutas. In the fourteenth century, it was annexed by the Faruqi rulers who ruled here till the sixteenth century. In 1599, Akbar's army occupied Burhanpur and it became the Mughal capital of Khandesh.

The city of Burhanpur was named after the famous Chisti saint Khwaja Burhanuddin Gharib (d. 1344 CE). Perhaps that is why there are many dargahs in the city. One of the most famous dargah is of Hazrat Nizamuddin Shah Bhikari. The dargah of Shah Bhikhari dates back to the reign of the Farooqi ruler Adil Khan II in the fifteenth century. Just like other dargahs, this is the resting place of many people. But the unique aspect of this dargah is that it sits on the riverbed of the Utawali River. More than a lakh devotees offer namaz on Barawafat—the Prophet's birthday and also the day of Shah Bhikhari's *urs*.

The other famous dargah is the luminous Dargah-e-Hakimi, an important pilgrimage for the Bohra community, the resting place of Syedna Abdul Tayeb Zakiuddin (d. 1787). He was the forty-first Da'i al-Mutlaq (head) of the Dawoodi Bohra sect of Muslims.

Another very important place of pilgrimage is the Gurudwara Badi Sangat. It marks the site where Guru Gobind Singh, travelling to the south with Emperor Bahadur Shah I, stayed in May–June 1708 and has a copy of Sri Guru Granth Sahib handwritten by the tenth Sikh Guru, Guru Gobind Singh Ji.

∞

The Faruqi rulers have left many architectural gems in the city and the Jama Masjid is a glorious testimony to their legacy. This mosque is special for it is proof of our syncretic culture with its Sanskrit and Arabic inscription on the walls, detailing its building by the Farooqi rulers. The mosque has no roof and its soaring arches fuse together to form a ceiling.

The Farooqi rulers also built a Shahi Qila or royal fort on the banks of the Tapti River. The Mughals used this Qila as their residence once Khandesh became a part of the Mughal Empire. The importance of the subah or province of Khandesh can be seen from the fact that Mughal princes, including Akbar's son Daniyal, Shah Jahan and Aurangzeb were its governors.

The *shikaar*-loving, pleasure-seeking Prince Daniyal built an Aahukhana, or deer park, opposite the Badshahi Qila in the village of Zainabad on the banks of the river Tapti. It was here that the young Aurangzeb met Zainabadi Bai and fell passionately in love with her. Unfortunately, their love story was doomed as Zainabadi Bai died soon after due to poisoning.

When Shah Jahan was the governor of the Deccan, he added various buildings within the Badshahi Qila, including a once-gorgeous and now deteriorating *hammam*, for his wife's relaxation. The hammam is beautifully painted and one of the fading frescoes has a building which looks remarkably like the Taj Mahal. It was in this palace that Mumtaz Mahal died on the night of 16–17 June 1631, after giving birth to Gauhar Ara Begum.

∞

Death plays a huge role in this city's history, if the beautiful tombs dotting the city are anything to go by. I came here in search of Mumtaz Mahal's original grave but was fascinated by the numerous other graves that dot the landscape.

The tomb of Shahnawaz Khan, son of Abdur Rahim Khan-e-Khana, is called 'Kala Taj Mahal' or 'Black Taj Mahal' by the locals. It's a beautiful monument, shaped like the Taj though built on a much smaller scale. And though it owes its name to the local black stones used for its construction, it has also been blackened by age.

I visited another stunning mausoleum, the grave of Bilqis

Begum—wife of Shah Shuja, son of Shah Jahan. Coincidently, she too died during childbirth, like Mumtaz Mahal.

It is very small but gorgeous, like the twelve-leaved, lotus-shaped platform it sits on. Its dome and walls are fluted which also gives it another name: Kharbooza Mahal or Kharbooze ka Gumbad.

In a village, some 10 kilometres away from Burhanpur, there is the *chhatri* of Raja Jai Singh, the great Rajput general who was the commander of the Mughal forces in the Deccan. He died at Burhanpur, reportedly while returning from the Deccan, and Aurangzeb built a chhatri in commemoration, keeping with the custom among the Rajputs.

It is a rarely visited monument and I am not surprised since the road leading to it, which goes through villages, is rough and not metalled. The chhatri itself is of black stone and looks quite grand, standing all alone amongst the plantain fields.

Coming back to the reason why I went to Burhanpur—in search of memories of Mumtaz Mahal.

Mumtaz Mahal was the granddaughter of I'timad-ud-Daulah the famous Persian immigrant, who had entered Mughal services and achieved a high rank. Her father was Asaf Khan and her aunt was the famous empress, Nur Jahan.

Her birth name was Arjumand Banu and she was engaged to be married to Prince Khurram, the favourite son of Emperor Jahangir, in April 1607 in Lahore. She was 14 years old at the time and the prince who ruled the Mughal Empire later as Shah Jahan was 15 years old. However, Khurram's first marriage was a diplomatic alliance arranged by Emperor Jahangi to the daughter of a Safavid noble Mirza Muzaffar Husain in December 1609.

It was only in May 1612 that Khurram's marriage was solemnized with Arjumand Bano. The Prince was very happy with his new wife and as his official biographer Qazwini writes, 'finding her in appearance and character elect [Mumtaz] among all the women of the time, he gave her the title Mumtaz Mahal Begum (Chosen One of the Palace), on the one hand that it might be a source of pride for that Chosen One of the Age'.[3]

Khurram himself got the title Shah Jahan from Jahangir only in 1617.

Though Shah Jahan had remarried, he was only attached to Mumtaz Mahal and she was his true companion, mentally, emotionally and physically. Qazwini writes,

> The mutual affection and harmony between the two had reached a degree never seen between a husband and wife of the class of rulers (sultan), or among the other people. And this was not merely out of sexual passion (hawa-yi-nafs): the excellent qualities, pleasing habits, outward and inward virtues, and spiritual and physical compatibility on both sides caused great love and affection, and extreme affinity and familiarity.[4]

She accompanied him everywhere, so it was natural that when Khan Jahan Lodi rebelled against the Mughal Empire, though she was pregnant, she accompanied him to Burhanpur to the same qila where it is said an image of a mausoleum was painted on the ceiling.

Recently, I saw a mirror case in the Freer Gallery of Art and Arthur M. Sackler Gallery in Washington D.C., made in 1628 for Shah Jahan with a painting of a heavily pregnant Mumtaz Mahal. She is glowing in the painting and that testifies to smooth pregnancies and childbirth. As this was her fourteenth pregnancy, both husband and wife could not have anticipated the complications that occurred. The Queen's condition deteriorated after she gave birth to Gauhar Ara and contemporary sources like Qazwini and Kanbo describe the Emperor's shock as she called him to bid farewell on the night of 16–17 June 1631. He wore white clothes, gave up listening to music, wearing jewellery and using perfumes for almost two years, and was perhaps one of the first Indians to wear spectacles because of constant weeping.

Mumtaz Mahal was laid to rest in the *Aahukhana*. A week later, Shah Jahan came to the Aahukhana and recited the *fateha* for his wife's soul and wept over her grave. He would come there to recite the fateha every Friday till he stayed in Burhanpur.

Locals tell me that Shah Jahan had initially decided to build a grand mausoleum for Mumtaz Mahal on the banks of the Tapti, but due to difficulties in transporting marble from Markana, Rajasthan, and the composition of the soil, he selected Agra. One local heritage enthusiast told me that the image of the mausoleum would not fall on the Tapti as the river was too narrow, so the idea was abandoned. Unfortunately, logistics stole Burhanpur's place in history and bestowed it on Agra.

Whatever the reasons for building the Rauza-e-Munawwara (the original name of the Taj Mahal) in Agra, the Aahukhana beckoned me. It seemed like I was part of the minority though, with only a few heritage lovers, who are fighting to preserve their city's heritage.

The Aahukhana, where Mumtaz Mahal's body lay for six months before being transported to Agra, used to be a huge area on the banks of river Tapti which included the village of Zainabad.

Today, it's the name given to a small portion which lies in the middle of nowhere with a dirt track leading to it. There are two buildings in the Aahukhana that are supposed to have been the queen's grave. One is the *baradari* in the fenced compound known today as Aahukhana and the other is a building with a tank in the centre and a mosque attached to it.

The baradari is within an enclosed compound. Its boundary wall and iron gates are worse for wear, with the walls breaking up in quite a number of places. There is wild overgrown grass and a dirty dry tank, which was once a source of delight for visitors to the garden. The pleasure palace built in front of it is now a place which brings displeasure: it is dirty, dank, smelly and covered in graffiti.

The baradari has long since lost its roof. Its beautiful columns sag under the burden of sorrow. They have been roughly propped up by bricks to prevent further destruction. It is a picture of desolation.

I was taken by my guides to another ruinous building a little further away from the baradari complex that was also a part of the original Aahukhana. It has a small tank and mosque. The guides told me that this was the site where Mumtaz Mahal was given her ritual funeral bath.

Burhanpur heritage enthusiasts claim this is the actual grave. Shahzada Asif, a resident who is said to have identified this place, observes Mumtaz Mahal's urs every year on 7 June in this place. Hoshang Havaldar, a local hotel owner and heritage enthusiast, described the urs to me. I stayed in his hotel and we spent the evenings bemoaning the state of Burhanpur's deteriorating heritage.

This building has no boundary wall and cotton farming is being done on its grounds. A rusted, decrepit board with barely distinguishable letters outside it proclaims in Hindi that this is 'Begum Mumtaz Mahal ki Qabr'.

On 1 December 1631, Mumtaz Mahal's body was taken out of the baradari and sent with ceremony to Agra, accompanied by her son Shah Shuja, her lady-in-waiting Sati-un-Nisa and Hakim Alimuddin Wazir Khan. They arrived in Agra 20 days later.

A special place was earmarked for her coffin in the grounds near the mosque area. It still exists. There were walls all around it so as to preserve her *purdah* even in death.

There are many theories of how her body was embalmed. Some say it was kept in a sealed lead and copper coffin filled with natural embalming herbs as per Unani techniques. Since the coffin was never opened, one doesn't know the state of decomposition or preservation of the queen's body.

But whatever state she may be sleeping in, in her grave in Taj Mahal, I am sure her soul cries at the wilderness that is the Aahukhana today.

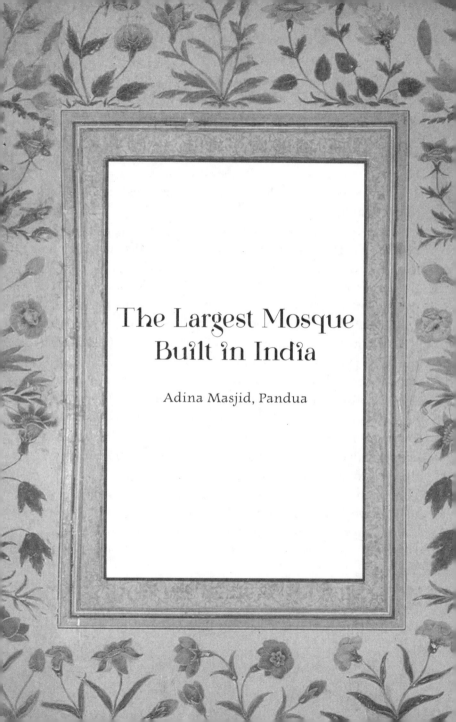

The Largest Mosque
Built in India

Adina Masjid, Pandua

The first time I heard about Lakhnauti (now Gaur) was in connection with Delhi's first Islamic tomb at Sultan Ghari. It was built by Sultan Iltutmish for his beloved son and heir, Nasiruddin Mahmud who died in 1299 while serving as the governor of Bengal. Lakhnauti was the capital. At that time, it seemed a distant dream that I would ever visit that area. But sometimes dreams do come true and a few years later, I was standing in the area that used to be called Lakhnauti.

Lakshmanavati, as Lakhnauti was known originally, was ruled by the Palas and then the Senas. King Lakshmana Sena laid Gaur's foundations and made it his capital in 1179. Sultan Iltutmish's general, Bakhtiyar Khilji, defeated him in 1202 and Lakhnauti became the provincial capital of the Delhi Sultanate. The hold of the Delhi Sultanate didn't survive for long and in 1342, Shamsuddin Ilyas Shah (1342–57) rebelled against Muhammad bin Tughlaq, the Delhi sultan, and declared his independence. The Ilyas Shahi dynasty was established and to complete the break with Delhi, the new sultan of Bengal shifted his capital from Lakhnauti to Pandua on the banks of the Mahananda River. Bengal was acknowledged as an independent sultanate which flourished till the sixteenth century.

Pandua served as the capital of the Ilyas Shahi Dynasty till the river shifted its course, but even after the capital was shifted back to Gaur by Sultan Nasiruddin Mahmud Shah (1435–59), it remained a mint town until the time of Sher Shah Suri.

Various rulers from the Ilyas Shahi, the house of Raja Ganesh, Habshi dynasty and the Hussain Shahi dynasty ruled from 1338 onwards till it was absorbed in the Mughal Empire in 1576 after the defeat of Daud Khan Karrani at the hands of Khan Jahan Quli, the general of Emperor Akbar.

Once a very well-planned city with markets and beautiful buildings, Gaur or Gouda, today, is quiet, dusty and ruined. In fact, the city was so beautiful that Humayun named it Jannatabad (city of heaven) for, to him, Gaur sounded like *gor* in Persian which means a grave.

The nearest town is Malda and has a few hotels where tourists who come to visit Gaur and Pandua stay. Malda district is situated on the juncture of the Mahananda and the Ganga and most of its monuments were built near it. It is an overnight train journey from Kolkata but well worth it, for both these medieval cities hide treasures in their bosom, lying forsaken under the hot sun. They lie to the north and south of Malda. For me it was an emotional journey, for I was moved by the beauty and majesty of the temples, mosques and dargahs and in tears at the sheer neglect of it all.

In *Memoirs of Gaur and Pandua*, Khan Sahib M. Abid Ali Khan quotes Spanish traveller João de Barros (1496–20 October 1570), who describes Gaur as: 'The population is so great and the streets so thronged with concourse and traffic of people, especially of such as come to present themselves at the king's court, that they cannot force their way past one another. A great part of the city consists of stately and well-wrought buildings.'[5]

After Sher Shah sacked it, the city decayed, and when the new cities of Murshidabad and English Bazar and later Calcutta came up—as was the custom of recycling in the medieval era—bricks and stones from here were carried in boats to the new constructions.

The first person to explore these spectacular ruins was

Henry Creighton, an indigo planter who lived near Gaur between 1786 and 1807. He made sketches of the fort and the palace.

After him, antiquarians Dr Franics Buchanan-Hamilton in 1808 and Major W. Franklin in 1810–11 left detailed descriptions of the ruins as they were at that time.

Islam came to Bengal in the thirteenth century with the governors of the Delhi Sultan but spread because of Shah Jalaluddin Tabrizi, the Suhrawardi saint who is still revered in the region. The place where he settled down was called Hazrat Pandua or revered Pandua as a mark of respect. Even today it is called Hazrat Pandua or Boro Pandua to distinguish it from another Pandua in the Hooghly district, which is known as Chota Pandua.

Various mosques were also built in this period. The beauty of the mosques built in this era by the sultans of Gaur was that they adapted to the local customs. Since stone was not available locally, we find mosques built of brick and decorated with terracotta ornamentation, which has made it susceptible to the vagaries of time and climate. The combination of domes, minarets and local elements such as terracotta, resulted in a very beautiful style of architecture.

There are many pretty, but ruined, mosques in Gaur, which was my first port of call. These are brick mosques with pretty terracotta designs on them. The local art of terracotta received a great push from being used on mosques. Of course today, we have exquisite terracotta temples where the artisans let artistic inspiration drive their process.

The next day I went to Pandua and nothing could have prepared me for the sheer size and desolate grandeur of the Adina Mosque there.

Adina Mosque

The Adina Masjid was built by Sultan Sikander Shah in 1374–75. The size of the Masjid (external: 565 by 317 feet) was to accommodate the thousands of worshippers in the new capital. An inscription which proclaims Sikandar Shah the sultan of Arabia and Persia, dates it to 1375.

If the size of the mosque was a message to the Delhi Sultan that the Bengal Sultan was here to stay, then it was certainly conveyed, as it was much larger, grander and majestic than the Begumpur Mosque built by Muhammad bin Tughlaq. The latter's grand gateway was missing and we entered through a small arched opening in the eastern side. This must have been for the public to enter, the smaller doors on the west being reserved for royalty and the imam.

The word, 'Adina' means Friday and Adina Masjid is another name for Jama Masjid or place of congregational prayers. It was the largest mosque in India at the time of its construction and as much a political statement of power (a message to the Delhi sultans perhaps) as a religious endeavour. Today Taj-ul-Masajid of Bhopal is the largest Indian mosque.

Since there was no main central dome and the smaller domes on the bays have mostly collapsed, all one can see are very tall walls with four circular, stone-faced turrets on all four corners. The size can be judged from the exterior, by its walls, but once I entered through its normal-sized door, I was overwhelmed. It is built in the traditional hypostyle, the type prevailing under the Delhi sultans in the north.

The approach to it is fairly underwhelming since there are no grand doorways, especially in such a grand mosque.

Cunningham, in his report, writes that the real entrance may have been at the

> south-east corner of the cloisters where the three archways at the eastern end of the south cloister are left open so that the people would enter at once into the south and the east cloister from the outside. As this arrangement utterly spoils the symmetry of the building, it was most probably an afterthought when the single small door in the middle of the east side was found utterly insufficient.[6]

The Adina Masjid has two parts, the *iwan* and the *sahen*. It is supposed to have been modelled on the Umayyad Mosque in Damascus. I have visited that too and it's indeed a covered-hypostyle, rectangular mosque. Another mosque built on the same architectural style was the Begumpur Masjid in Delhi, built in 1387 by the minister of Firuz Shah Tughlaq and could have provided inspiration for not only the design but ambition to surpass in size.

The door of the Adina opens directly into the western gallery with its pillars and though it is dark, its grandeur seems to affect all those inside. A series of arches, built on short, powerful pillars with square plinths and weighty block capitals, greet the visitor. This lofty main hall measures 64 by 33 feet. On each side it has five arched openings, which lead to the courtyard.

The first feature that strikes and attracts all visitors is a simple wooden staircase leading up to an upper floor in the northern part of the mosque, called Badshah ka Takht, which was obviously reserved for the sultan and the women of his family. As I saw many women exiting down the stairs from it, I decided to retrace their steps. This was the private area reserved in the mosque for the sultan and the royal ladies. Today there is a lot of debate on whether women are allowed in mosques in India, but if we study medieval Indian mosques, starting from Quwwatul Islam mosque in Delhi, most medieval Jama Masjid had an upper/side chamber reserved for the king and the royal women.

This is the best preserved and the most ornamented area of the Adina. Though today, the flooring is wooden in most places, the presence of stone slabs in some places shows that it must have been all stone at one point in time. This is vaulted with six bays each in front of three *mihrabs* forming a total of 18 bays. The pillars which bear the weight of the dome are black basalt, from which brick arches soar up to form domed ceilings with the help of squinches. The mihrabs in this section are made of stone and decorated with Quranic verses in tughra calligraphy and the floral designs along with it are exquisite.

The arabesque and geometrical ornamentation on the mihrabs here showcase the fluidity of Indo-Islamic architecture, with the Indian artisans bringing with them their motifs and designs while adapting to the technical specifications.

When I compare my memories and photographs (taken in 2018) with a painting by Sita Ram made in 1817,[7] there is a definite loss of surface decorations on the vaulted part in this chamber. The structure however, stands strong.

There is a now roofless room (42 sq. feet) attached to this *takht* on the western side, which is popular with tourists, especially couples who like to sit on the parapets. This is said to have been the sultan's private chamber and Sikandar Shah was supposed to have been buried here. Unfortunately, when the roof collapsed, all signs of a grave disappeared. The Sita Ram (worked c. 1810–22) painting in the British Library shows the exterior of the Masjid. It is an idealized design and shows 'the ruins of the tomb of Sikandar Shah along the western wall'.[8]

The inscription describing the construction of this mosque in 1375 by Sikandar Shah is placed on the back wall of the takht.

From here I came down and once again entered the open courtyard (445 by 168 sq. feet). Surrounded by covered galleries with arched and domed bays on all four sides, there are around 260 pillars and 370 domed bays in total.

The longer side of the galleries run north to south. The main prayer hall galleries are five bays deep while the other three sides are three-bayed.

The mihrabs (41 in total) on the western wall are made of black basalt with carving, while the tympanum is brick, decorated with terracotta and is exquisite. While the side mihrabs remain more or less similar, each tympanum is differently ornamented with terracotta designs and one can only imagine its beauty when it was used as a Jama Masjid under the sultans. One common motif is the lamp, inspired by the Surah an-Nur of the Quran and censers on the mihrabs, as use of incense sticks is popular in mosques. The geometrical patterns, motifs, terracotta rosettes and abstract arabesque designs on the walls, pillars and mihrabs of the mosque are breathtaking.

To the right of the main prayer hall are the pulpit and the central mihrab.

The *mimbar* next to the main mihrab is also made of black basalt with *sang-e-musa* steps leading up to it. This is the place from where the Imam would give his sermon every Friday before the prayers.

The presence of Hindu and Buddhist gods and motifs on the steps of the pulpit as well as the walls of the mosque show that the stones used in the mosque were from earlier Hindu and Buddhist buildings. The *kirtimukha* on one of the steps of the mimbar is exquisite and must have adorned a temple nearby, before it was destroyed.

On the reuse of material Richard Eaton writes:

Although its builders reused a good deal of carved stone from pre-conquest monuments, the mosque does not appear to have been intended to convey a message of political subjugation to the region's non-Muslims, who in any event would not have used the structure. In fact, stylistic motifs in the mosque's prayer niches reveal the builders' successful adaptation, and even appreciation, of late Pala-Sena art.[9]

It takes quite a while to walk around the whole mosque and enjoy its ruined beauty but is well worth it.

There were many visitors when I was there but majority of them were locals. Each mihrab and the terracotta designs above it needs to be savoured and paid tribute to. As I stood there, drinking in its beauty, I couldn't stop myself from thinking that a monument of such beauty deserves to be celebrated by many more. It is indeed 'one of the most ambitious architectural plans ever conceived and executed in the Indian subcontinent'.[10]

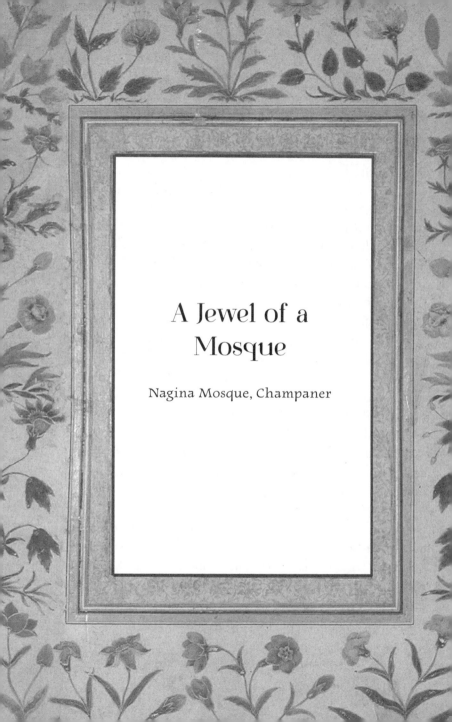

A Jewel of a Mosque

Nagina Mosque, Champaner

Gujarat was always a very rich province with its geographical proximity to sea routes, its fertile land and temperate climate. It was ruled by various dynasties, including the Maurya, Gupta, Maitraka, Solanki and Chalukyas. Its riches and strategic location soon attracted Alauddin Khilji, the Delhi sultan, and Gujarat became a part of the Delhi Sultanate in 1297.

In 1398, when the Delhi Sultanate was reeling under Timur's attack, Zafar Khan, the governor of Gujarat, declared independence and laid the foundation of the Muzaffarid dynasty after his regnal name Muzaffar Shah I. His successor Ahmad Shah laid the foundation of Ahmedabad and built some magnificent mosques and structures there.

Mahmud Shah I (1458–1511), also known as Mahmud Begada, after his achievement of having conquered two *garh* (Pavgadh and Junagarh forts) shifted his capital to Pavagadh and founded a new city called Mahmudabad in Champaner.

The architecture of Gujarat was highly developed and had a unique style. The Modhera Temple built by the Solanki rulers, with its rich stone carvings, is a glorious testimony to the artistic perfection of the artisans.

When the local architecture was blended with Islamic architecture, it produced the most outstanding and exquisite minarets with the tree of life carved on them.

The tree of life or *kalpavriksha* is a dominant artistic theme in Hindu, Jain and Buddhist mythology and cosmology as a wish-fulfilling divine tree. It is also an artistic theme in many Islamic artworks and monuments as Shajarat-al Khuld or the Tree of Immortality. It is this tree which is mentioned in the Quran as being present in the Garden of Eden and forbidden to Adam and Eve. A tree of life and a tree of knowledge about good and evil is mentioned in the Book of Genesis as well.

So it is not surprising that when the Muslim sultanate of Gujarat started its construction activities, the local artisans and stone carvers incorporated the tree of life into the mosques they built for the new rulers, as it encapsulated the commonality in different faiths. In North India, it was the lotus that had been adopted and adapted in the domes of tombs and mosques. This fusion of ideas and themes is what gave birth to Indo-Islamic architecture.

James Fergusson writes, 'Of the various forms which the Saracenic architecture assumed in India, that of Ahmadabad may probably be considered as the most elegant, as it certainly is the most characteristic of all. No other form is so essentially Indian, and no one tells its tale with the same unmistakable distinctness.' [11]

After a few thoroughly enjoyable days soaking in the architecture of Ahmedabad, we left for Champaner. It can be reached from Ahmedabad but if one is travelling specifically to see that erstwhile capital city, then Vadodara is the closest city, which is 45 kilometres from Champaner.

The tree of life on the windows of the Sidi Saiyyed mosque in Ahmedabad is famous all over the world and was adapted by IIM Ahmedabad as their logo. The tree of life on the Ahmedabad Jama Masjid built by Ahmed Shah I also deserves a special mention. The list also includes other city monuments such as the Rani Sipri Masjid built by Rani Sipri, the wife of Mahmud Begada in 1472, Muhafiz Khan Masjid, built by a noble of the same name in the court of Mahmud Begada in 1485 and the Rani Rupmati mosque.

The Sarkhej Roza, shrine of the Sufi saint Shaikh Ahmed

Ganj Bakhsh, on whose suggestion Ahmad Shah established his new capital on the banks of the river Sabarmati, is also worth a visit. Don't forget to look at the ceilings in every building in that region. Since Sarkhej (the name comes from *sarkhez* or fertile) was home to indigo dyers, the ceiling is painted in indigo and is extremely evocative of the relationship a Sufi saint would have with his followers.

Coming back to Champaner, the first place one visits here is the magnificent Jama Masjid. Another exquisite structure with its intricate *jaalis*, mihrabs and carvings.

As my attention was on the mihrab design, I wasn't looking at the top and would have missed an elaborately carved tree of life on the ceiling, right in front of the central mihrab, had my guide not told me to slow down. He pointed it out to me and told me to stand still, close my eyes and feel the peace. And indeed, I did.

Many devotees come to Pavagadh. As per Hindu tradition, the hill was formed on the spot where the right toe of the Goddess Sati, a previous incarnation of Goddess Kali, fell on earth. In Sanskrit and Gujarati literature, the drama *Gangadasa Pratapa Vilasa Natakam* and the garba of Kalika describes this town. The temple of Kalikamata on the hill has many devotees who come to visit it.

The tenth-century Lakulisa temple on the hill dedicated to Lord Shiva, though now in ruins, is a very beautiful temple with intricate carvings. A Jain group of temples belonging to the Digamber sect is also located on the hill.

∞

The Khichi branch of Chauhan Rajputs ruled Pavagadh. When Mahmud Begada attacked the fort, Patai Rawal, the Khichi ruler, asked the sultan of Malwa, Sultan Ghiyasuddin, for help. However, Mahmud Begada prevailed and after defeating Patai Rawal he established his new capital at its foothills in 1483 in Champaner, calling it Mahmudabad. The sultan gave permanent landholdings to his courtiers in his new capital to encourage their investment in developing the land.

The new capital flourished till 1534 when the Mughal emperor Humayun attacked it. Bahadur Shah, the then sultan of Gujarat, shifted the capital to Ahmedabad. Champaner stayed in the hands of the Mughals till 1727.

After that, Champaner kept changing hands and after a brief possession by the Scindias, it was handed over to the British in 1853.

The beautiful city with its incredible architecture had fallen into ruins after Humayun's attack. According to the *Gazetteer of Bombay Presidency,* this fertile land embellished with good streets, squares and whitewashed houses of stones had only become ruinous and

in 1554, its only points of interest were fine banyan trees, large fruit-eating bats and thorny brushwood. Like the rest of Gujarat it suffered from the disorders of the next twenty years (1554–74). But unlike Ahmedabad and Surat the establishment of law and order under the Emperor Akbar (1573–1605) brought Champaner no return of prosperity. At the beginning of the seventeenth century its air was weakening, its water poisonous, and its orchards and gardens the lair of the tiger and lion. Its buildings had fallen in ruins, and its people had given their goods to the winds of destruction. Instead of flowers were thorns, and instead of gardens close-knotted brushwood, and of its sandal groves neither the name nor the trace was left. It showed the truth of the verse, 'All on earth fades and God does as he wills'.[12]

The British retrieved the monuments from the overgrowth and the jungle that had grown in and around it. Today the area is the Champaner-Pavagadh Archaeological Park and is a UNESCO World Heritage Site.

Mirat-i-Sikandari describes Champaner as a place which attracted people from far and wide during Mahmud Begada's reign because of its pleasure pavilions and gardens but alas! These pleasure gardens designed by a Persian architect from Khorasan and the pavilions now lay in ruin.[13]

Roads were built to the Kevda and Nagina mosques but since not many visitors go there, they are now more like narrow dirt tracks in the middle of the fields.

Most visitors to Champaner visit the Jama Masjid, the fort on Pavagadh Hill and the ancient temples. A few visit the fort area that is close to the Jami Masjid.

Since I had read up beforehand, I knew that there were hidden gems in the area, especially one called Nagina Masjid (Jewel Mosque), built during the reign of Mahmud Begada. It is on the north side and hidden deep inside. One has to go through the fort to its southern side and exit from it on to some overgrown and dirt roads to be able to reach the mosque, but believe me, it is worth it.

The main attraction of the Champaner mosques is its exquisite geometrical and arabesque designs. The mihrabs are beautifully decorated with flower, chain, pot and foliage motifs. As in the Ahmedabad mosques, the minarets which flank either side of the main prayer hall of the mosque are ornamented with the tree of life and other designs.

The Champaner mosques follow the trabeate rather than arcuate style of architecture.

In the middle of the fields, stands the Nagina Masjid on a high plinth. It is quite a large structure with seven arches. The tall central arch is flanked on each side by the minarets and there are three smaller ones on each side.

A photograph from 1869[14] shows that the minarets were intact though covered with vegetation. The British Library describes it as, 'The central dome had already fallen in when this photograph was taken.'

However, when I was there in 2018, the domes were very much present, while the minarets had fallen down and were only intact till roof level. Further examination of the photographs leads me to conclude that what is being called the Nagina Masjid in the British Library photographs is today labelled as Kevada Mosque, which is also nearby. The Kevada Mosque has both its minarets intact (cleaned of vegetation) and a dome-less interior chamber.

What I am describing is the mosque complex currently described as Nagina Masjid by the ASI and called a, 'small ruined mosque to the north-west of the Nagina Masjid, Champaner' on the British Library site.[15]

In the main hall of the Nagina Masjid, stone columns dominate. There is a high-domed ceiling with an open space to let the light and air enter with a carved stone railing running around on the upper level. There are three central mihrabs (which point to the direction of Kaaba for the faithful to pray). These mihrabs have a floral design, very reminiscent to me of antique *kundan* earrings. Perhaps, the workers had borrowed inspiration from them.

Floral designs decorate the niches in the lower portion too.

There are three domes and 10 cupolas supported on 80 decorative columns.

As in the Jami Masjid and others, the sidewalls of the mosque on its northern and southern sides have a carved *jharokha* at its centre.

Volume three of the 1887 *Gazetteer of the Bombay Presidency* describes the mosque as having been of pure white stone. Today it is a sun-kissed pale yellow but one can imagine how a pure white mosque would have gotten its present name. It is indeed a pearl. The gazetteer also mentions the plenitude of mangoes in its gardens and orchards as well as sandalwood trees growing so freely that people used it to build houses.

There is no ablution tank but the gazetteer mentions a large brick well, spanned by a stone arch, which must have been used for the purpose of ablution before prayers.

Attractive as the mosque is, a nearby, unknown cenotaph on its grounds is what takes your breath away with its outstanding carvings.

Its panels on the doorjambs, depicting the tree of life, are exquisite. Tiny jharokhas built high up on the outer walls also have a fine tree of life carving on it. The dome has fallen down and with it perhaps the grave that it must have once contained.

James Burgess describes it in the *Archaeological Survey of Western India Volume VI* as,

> Among those remains still found in the forest, attention
> may be drawn to the ruin of what must have been one

of the most ornately carved tombs in Gujarat... The dome has fallen in and the whole is a mere shell. It is not at all large, and had only one arched entrance on each side, with a blind arch on both sides of these entrances. The upper portions of these blind arches were ornamented with niches such as are common on the bases and by other rich carving; but the pilasters at the corners and jambs of the doorways are carved in patterns of the richest designs. Except the two famous windows in the Sidi Sayyid's mosque at Ahmadabad there is hardly anything elsewhere to match these twelve pillars in richness and variety of decoration.[16]

I tend to agree with Burgess, for the workmanship is breathtaking. I spent a good hour savouring the ornamentation on the tomb. I wish I had had more time and hope to go again soon.

When I compare the photograph taken in 1885 with the ones I took, I can see the restoration work undertaken by the ASI, as the former is in quite a ruinous condition. I am glad that this jewel of a tomb has been restored for us to enjoy and pay homage to the workmanship of the old.

The photographs of the mosque, too, show a ruined platform and vegetation. Today it may be deserted but it is in a well-restored and well-maintained condition. I am glad to say that the forested land shown in the 1885 photograph is still intact.

Since a huge number of tourists are usually on the lookout for selfie points, let me add that the open arches are a perfect location for taking selfies and photographs!

The Secrets that Khusrau Bagh Hides in Its Heart

Allahabad

Allahabad or Prayagraj, as it has been recently renamed, has a long and glorious history. It is one of the holiest cities of India and the site of the confluence of the two sacred rivers, Ganga and Yamuna. The annual Kumbh Mela on the banks of the Ganges witnesses lakhs of devotees, who visit for taking a holy dip in the river.

It was also the site of Akbar's largest fort and the capital of his 16 subahs. Akbar's administrative reforms are very famous and glimpses of many of his revenue and administrative reforms can still be seen in our structures today. One of them was to create 16 subahs of Ilahbas, with Ilahbas as its capital. In 1583, he laid the foundation stone and the Ilahbas fort came up. According to contemporary chroniclers like Badauni, when Akbar was informed about the devotion of the Hindus for the sacred site of Sangam (the confluence of the two holy rivers) and their wish to die there (as death there would mingle their soul with the spirit of God), he instantly decided to name the place as Ilahbas—the abode of God!

Another reason given for the name Ilahbas is that Ila is actually the mother of Pururavas, the progenitor of the Aila tribe. The Mahabharata mentions the name also as a river (variously identified) or as a king. Vas means abode, so the new city was named Abode of Ila. Prayag was the name of the area where yagna or pooja was done at the Sangam. Prayag was not renamed, instead, a new city was created.

During the reign of Shahjahan, it became popular as Ilahabad. The British started referring to it as Allahabad, the city of Allah. It became an administrative capital of the British and prospered under them.

The Allahabad University has produced many famous scholars and professors.

Its parks, gardens and colonial buildings are very famous as is Anand Bhavan, the home of Motilal Nehru, which is now a museum.

Apart from all these riches, there was another magnet for me in Allahabad—the treasures that hide in Khusrau Bagh.

The garden and its tombs have been captured for posterity in the paintings of Thomas and William Daniell entitled, 'Oriental Scenery'. The four tombs inside have been well preserved and while there are now grass lawns and not trees, it is still easily comparable to Daniells' paintings.

The main Chunar sandstone gateway of Khusrau Bagh is on the western side. The recessed entrance arch has a wooden door which, though dilapidated, is still holding fort. The bastions and side galleries are now hidden by shops, as the gateway opens into the market and a part of it was demolished for widening the road in 2019. However, one can see the remnants of the glory the Daniells made famous in their 1802 painting. This lofty gateway of Khusrau Bagh was made under the charge of Aqa Reza who was Jahangir's principal artist in the Allahabad court. The gateway has an inscription dated to 1606–7 which reads: 'this lofty edifice was completed by Aqa Reza, the painter, a devoted official of the emperor.'[17]

The regular entry is from another plain and sturdy gateway. One can enter through either gateway into a spacious park with guava trees, guavas sellers and rose gardens.

Khusrau Bagh is very popular with morning walkers, people doing yoga and children playing around. Most are not concerned with the four tombs located there and very few are acquainted with its tragic history. But before we enter the park, let us travel back in time to 1605–6.

'Who thought that this boy of few years
Would behave so badly to his sire?
At the first taste of the cup he brings up the lees.
He melts away my glory and his own modesty.
He sets on fire the throne of Khūrshīd,
He longs for the place of Jamshīd.'[18]

This is Jahangir, talking about his son Khusrau Mirza's rebellion against him in *Tuzuk-e-Jahangiri*.

Futile ideas had entered the mind of Khusrau in consequence of his youth and the pride youths have, and the lack of experience and the lack of foresight of worthless companions, especially at the time of my revered father's illness. Some of these short-sighted ones, through the multitude of their crimes and offences, had become hopeless of pardon and indulgence, and imagined that by making Khusrau a tool they might conduct the affairs of State through him. They overlooked the truth that acts of sovereignty and world rule are not things to be arranged by the worthless endeavours of defective intellects. The just Creator bestows them on him whom he considers fit for this glorious and exalted duty, and on such a person doth He fit the robe of honour.

He who is seized of Fortune cannot be deprived of it;
Throne and diadem are not things of purchase;
It is not right to wrest crown and dominion
From the head which God, the Crown-cherisher, has indicated.

A Saint, a Folk Tale and Other Stories

My trouble was this, that my son without any cause or reason should become an opponent and an enemy. If I should make no endeavour to capture him, the fractious or rebellious would have an instrument, or else he would take his own way and go for an asylum to the Ūzbegs or the Persians, and contempt would fall upon my government.[19]

Khusrau Mirza (16 August 1587–26 January 1622) was the eldest son of Emperor Jahangir and his Rajput wife Man Bai, daughter of Raja Bhagwant Das, the ruler of Amer. On Khusrau's birth, Man Bai was given the title of Shah Begum.

As Jahangir writes in the *Tuzuk*, 'My first marriage and that at the commencement of my adolescence was with her. After Khusrau's birth I gave her the title of Shāh Begam.'

Emperor Akbar and some of his courtiers saw Prince Salim, Akbar's only surviving son, as indolent and uninterested in the matters of state. But Salim's eldest son, Khusrau, was not only Akbar's favourite but also greatly liked by the courtiers and the public. Not surprisingly, Akbar's trusted general and Khusrau's uncle, Man Singh, and his foster brother, Aziz Koka, who was Khusrau's father in law, wanted the popular Khusrau to succeed the emperor. But these plans came to naught when Akbar lay dying on his bed. Salim managed to enter the emperor's bedchamber (Akbar's senior wives favoured him) and as Akbar's gaze fell on his son, he feebly handed over the royal turban and robe to him.

On November 1605, Jahangir ascended the throne. Khusrau and his wife (Aziz Koka's daughter) were placed under house arrest in the Agra Fort.

On 15 April 1606, Khusrau left Agra Fort with 350 horsemen, who were his adherents, on the pretext of visiting his grandfather's mausoleum in Sikandra.

He was joined by a few other nobles. Jahangir acted with a surprising energy and Dilawar Khan, the newly appointed governor, sealed off Lahore before he could reach. On 27 April 1606, within 12 days of him having left Agra Fort, Khusrau was defeated on the banks of river Ravi, near Lahore, and brought back in chains before his father. After being disgraced, he was imprisoned in the Agra Fort where he was blinded. Later, a remorseful Jahangir sent his physicians to restore his son's sight and though complete sight could not be restored, he didn't live in utter darkness.

His support in the Mughal court remained, for after all he was the nephew of Raja Man Singh and son-in-law of Aziz Koka. His younger brother Khurram, who later ascended the throne as Shah Jahan, always saw a threat in him and demanded his custody. In 1616, he was handed over to Asaf Khan, the brother of Nur Jahan and father-in-law of Khurram, as a compromise.

That Nur Jahan used him as a pawn to strengthen her hold over the Mughal throne didn't help his case. Empress Nur Jahan was a powerful personality during the later years of her husband Jahangir's reign. She saw Khurram as a threat and proposed a marriage between Khusrau and Ladli Begum, her daughter from her first husband. She promised to give him freedom. In a stroke, she could then neutralize Khurram. But the only support that Khusrau had after his rebellion was that of his wife, daughter of Aziz Koka. He refused to remarry despite his wife's pleas that he should gain his freedom and save his life. Khusrau remained steadfast and eventually Nur Jahan married her daughter to Jahangir's youngest son, Shahryar.

In 1620, Khusrau's custody was finally given to Prince Khurram. Khurram, wanting to eliminate all obstacles in the way to the throne, had him killed in Burhanpur in 1622.

Khusrau was buried in Burhanpur but on Jahangir's orders that he should be buried near his mother in Allahabad, his body was moved. While his coffin was being transported from Burhanpur to Allahabad, there were continuous and spontaneous bursts of affection from people, who stopped the cortège along the way. It is said that people had built shrines in his memory, which were later destroyed on Jahangir's orders.

A grand tomb was made for Khusrau in the Mughal garden in Allahabad, comissioned by his sister Sultan-un-Nisa Begum in the same garden where his mother was buried.

This garden today is named after the Prince but its earlier name, according to Finch, was Menepur. He mentions seeing Shah Begum's terraced tomb there.

All the tombs are kept locked to prevent vandalism since, unfortunately, we are very fond of scribbling our names on monuments.

Khusrau's tomb is the last in the garden and is normally kept locked and is in a slightly forlorn condition. Originally a wooden canopy covered his cenotaph and his personal copy of the Quran was kept beside him.

When it was first made, it must have been beautiful as it is painted with cypress and flowers. Cypress has always been associated with death and mourning. Though some of the paintings in the niches have been destroyed, one can get a sense of the splendour they must have once had. It has beautiful stone jaalis as *nur* was an important aspect of

Islam and light falling on the grave was essential. There are Persian verses inscribed on the doorways that reflect the tragedy of Khusrau Mirza's life.

There is another grave in the side chamber of Khusrau's tomb. Though according to legend it is his mare, I wonder if it might be his ill-fated son Dawar Baksh as is denoted by the *takhti* on the cenotaph. Asaf Khan crowned Dawar Baksh as a temporary emperor after Jahangir's death to keep the throne safe for his son-in-law Shah Jahan, who was was in the Deccan. As soon as Shah Jahan reached Kashmir, Dawar Baksh was executed.

Another tragic story is that of Shah Begum. She was a Kachhwaha princess, the daughter of Raja Bhagwant Das. She could not reconcile herself to the rift between her husband Jahangir and her son, and died on 16 May 1604 of an opium overdose. In *Tuzk-e-Jahangiri*, Jahangir writes:

> His [Khusrau's] mother, while I was prince, in grief at his ways and behaviour and the misconduct of her brother Mādho Singh, killed herself by swallowing opium (tiryāq). What shall I write of her excellences and goodness? She had perfect intelligence, and her devotion to me was such that she would have sacrificed a thousand sons and brothers for one hair of mine. She constantly wrote to Khusrau and urged him to be sincere and affectionate to me. When she saw that it was of no use and that it was unknown how far he would be led away, she from the indignation and high spirit, which are inherent in the Rajput character, determined upon death. Her mind was several times disturbed, for such feelings were hereditary, and her

ancestors and her brothers had occasionally showed signs of madness, but after a time had recovered. At a time when I had gone hunting, on Zīl-ḥijja 26th, 1013 [6 May 1605], she in her agitation swallowed a quantity of opium, and quickly passed away. It was as if she had foreseen this behaviour of her unworthy son.

Her tomb, in respect to her Rajput lineage, has been made in that style of architecture and to me seemed very similar to the Panch Mahal in Fatehpur Sikri which is also made of Chunar sandstone.

It was designed in 1606 by Aqa Reza, as a three-storeyed terraced tomb. As it was the first tomb to be built here, it is aligned with the grand gateway. Shah Begum's tomb does not give a date of construction and could have been built at around the same time as the gateway.

It is an interesting building and can be opened on prior request and permission by the ASI guards. Once you climb up to the top, you can see a false cenotaph in lonely splendour on the top of the building. It is like a Rajput chatri, the style of cenotaphs common for Rajput royal families.

As Asher interestingly noted, 'The basic plan of Shah Begum's tomb, in turn, seems to have been a prime source for the design of Akbar's tomb.'

The tomb is adorned by arabesque inscriptions designed by Mir Abdullah Mushkin Qalam, Jahangir's chief calligrapher. The long tombstone with Mushkin Qalam's calligraphy is very pretty and gives the date as well as describes the departed lady's virtues.

However, the most beautiful of these three tombs is that of Jahangir's daughter Sultan-un-Nisa Begum, which is in the middle, flanked by her mother and brother.

At the entrance itself, one can see that she inherited her father's penchant and eye for paintings.

The ceiling of the tomb is simply mind-blowing, conceived as a series of concentric stars with *muqarnas*. The original colours are beautifully preserved. It is easily one of the best-preserved tombs I have seen anywhere in India from this period.

However, she was not buried in it. She died on 4th Sha'ban 1056 (5 September 1646) and was, at her own request, buried in her grandfather's tomb at Sikandra. The crypt chamber is empty and is now a home to bats.

As this is a garden tomb, there is an intricate system of waterways with water flowing into channels to emphasize the concept of paradisiacal tombs. Waterways were always an important part of gardens and tombs as per the Islamic concept of Jannat.

In a corner of the garden, opposite the royal tombs, is another tomb said to be that of a 'servant' named Bibi Tamolan. Constructed in the first half of the seventeenth century, her tomb is built on an octagonal platform with a domed octagonal tomb chamber on top.

The historic importance of Khusrau Bagh didn't end with Khusrau. During the Revolt of 1857, Khusrau Bagh was the headquarters of Maulvi Liaqat Ali. He and his group of patriots fighting the British were defeated in two weeks and Khusrau Bagh was retaken from their control.

What seems like a park hides so many heroic and tragic histories!

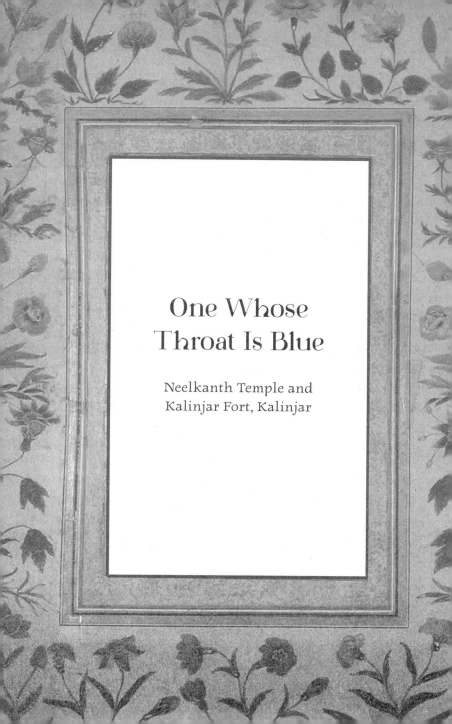

One Whose Throat Is Blue

Neelkanth Temple and
Kalinjar Fort, Kalinjar

> *One whose throat is blue*
> *I bow to Nīlakaṇṭha (who has) ten arms, three eyes,*
> *is sky clad [and] lord of the directions,*
> *dark eyed and adorned by/with poison.*

(Translation by Rohini Bakshi)[20]

One of the most famous legends is that of *samudra manthan* or churning of the oceans. This legend is described in the Bhagvata Purana, the Mahabharata and the Vishnu Purana.

This story is about the time when the gods and demons would fight and the demons often got the upper hand. The gods appealed to Lord Vishnu who advised them to solve the problem with diplomacy, which resulted in an alliance between the gods and the demons to churn the sea of milk for amrita, the nectar of immortality, which they would divide equally. Meanwhile, Lord Vishnu assured the gods that he would ensure they alone got the amrita.

During the churning, many objects came up and one was the *haalaa-hala*, a pot of very potent poison, which could destroy everyone. Again, on Lord Vishnu's advice the gods approached Lord Shiva who was the only one capable of swallowing it without being affected.

It is said that Lord Shiva swallowed the poison while his consort, Goddess Parvati, held his neck to prevent it from going into the stomach. It turned his throat blue, which is why he's called Neelkanth or blue throated.

Though the poison didn't harm him, his throat was burning and he came to earth to rest.

The place where he came to rest, according to legend, was Kalinjar.

Thus, this place came to be associated with Lord Shiva, the Neelkanth. The vedas mention it as a *tapasya sthana,* while it is mentioned in the Mahabharata, the reference is that of the famed mountain of Kalinjar and that whoever bathes in the lake of gods acquires the same merit that they would by giving away 1,000 cows.[21] The geographical location was perfect for ascetics as they could get protection from the elements, and from the overhanging rocks, in the caves of the hills.

This mountain was always associated with Shiv worship and a Chandela inscription refers to it as 'the dwelling place of Nilkantha (Lord Shiva): *nilakanthadhivasam kalanjarim.*'

There are enough epigraphs to suggest a pre-Chandela antiquity.

At least 10 inscriptions inside the fort belong to a period between seventh and tenth century. An inscription, probably dated to seventh century, on the Chandi Darwaza claims that the 'house of god Bhadresvara (i.e. temple) was constructed by a Pandava king named Udayana'. Another inscription (AD ninth century) records the construction of a temple (kirtti) of Shiva on the hill. From another epigraph it appears that by AD ninth century, the temple of Shiva, probably the Neelkanth Temple, had been established and was being visited by pilgrims.[22]

The cave with its lingam thus existed when the Chandelas captured the area. They are responsible for building the mandap and the exquisite carvings on the mountain rocks. 'The temple of Nilkantha probably was finally completed during the reign of Parmardideva. An inscription dated AD 28 October 1201 records an eulogy of this king as well as his eulogy for the deity.'[23]

The temple is below the ramparts and from the top, the 165 steps that lead down to it in a long and winding route look very daunting, but don't let that deter you as it is worth every bit of the effort. The entrance gateway to the temple is known as Parimardeva Darwaza, attributed to Raja Parmal (1167–1203).

Though the scenery that accompanies one down the steps is enough to refresh the tired feet, it's the first sight of the very Grecian-altar-looking 16-pillared yagna mandap from the top that is enough to fill one with a sense of purpose and we continued down with renewed vigour.

All along the route, there are carvings and statues on the rocks. In fact, at the museum of Kalinjar Fort, the ASI officer said that out of the 874 specimens of sculptures that they had, most were found during excavations of the temple and I can well believe him after seeing the riches still there.

A gateway leading to the village is guarded by an adorable life size Ganesha statue wearing ankle bells carved onto the pillar. On the rock, just a little way above the mandap, there are spectacular statues of Chamundi Devi.

The eight-columned mandap, which was covered once upon a time, now stands under the open sky as a testimony to time. Its corners were cut in such a way that it looks like an octagon. These columns are finely carved with dwarfish figures supporting a square abacus.

Behind the mandap is a small shrine cut into the rock itself with a 4-feet-6-inches-tall Shivaling of dark blue stone installed in it. The unique feature of the Shivaling is that it is always wet near the throat portion, even if there is a drought or famine in the area.

The door of the cave is a massive stone, shutter-like thing

which, the pujari told me, used to move, but they no longer know the secret lever. However, the exquisite carvings of goddesses Ganga and Yamuna on the doorjamb along with Lord Shiva and Parvati are fascinating.

To the right of the temple, a few steps down, there is the most amazing statue of Kal Bhairav (an incarnation of Lord Shiva) carved on a rock recess. It's easy to miss, as most people return from the mandap area and it is not visible from there.

It is 24 feet high, 17 feet wide and has 18 arms, wearing snake earrings and garlanded by skulls. The force and majesty of this statue is stunning and one can feel the power of destiny, which it is worshipped for. A snake garlands his torso. On the side is a much smaller four-feet figure of Goddess Kali.

Just above the temple is a natural water source that never dries up and water continually drips on to the Shivaling, keeping the neck moist. As many as 35 steps lead up to the sarovar, cutting in the mountains behind the temple.

Kalinjar lived up to its name, which means destroyer of time, and despite many attacks, it still stands strong. It is one of the few forts that repulsed the invasions of Mahmud Ghazni.

It was built on an isolated flat-topped hill, 1,340 feet above the plains in the Vindhya Range. The lower part of the hill was fairly easy to climb, the middle part was steep and the upper level, being perpendicular, was impossible to ascend, thus making it a perfect defensive fortress.

The saying 'so high that it impedes the progress of the sun at mid-day'[24] seems absolutely apt here.

The fort is aligned in an east-west direction and is almost a mile in length and half a mile in breadth. One requires physical fitness to climb to and back from the temple, though you can drive in your vehicle in the fort itself.

The fort is in the Banda district of UP, on the border of MP and falls in the village of Tarahati.

This area was held by the Gurjara Pratihara rulers of Kannauj in the ninth century, passing on to the Rashtrakutas in mid-tenth century. In AD 954, Kalinjar came into the hands of the Chandela rulers. Chandra Varma, a contemporary of Prithviraj Chauhan laid the foundations of a fort on this location. His son Madan Varma completed it.

Khwaja Nizamuddin Ahmad (1551–1621) writes in *Tabaqat-i-Akbari* that the fort of Kalinjar had 'no equal in the whole country of Hindustan for (its) strength and impregnability.'

The fort had a chequered history, falling into the hands of Qutbuddin Aibak in 1202, then being retaken by the Bundelas in 1210–11. It was in the control of the Baghelas of Gwalior, who held it in the sixteenth century until Humayun besieged it.

In 1544, Sher Shah Suri attacked it, and though he was victorious, he was killed there in 1545 in an accident. A live rocket hit the hill and fell on a powder magazine near which Sher Shah was standing. He died of the burns. The Shah was given a temporary burial in the fort before his body was shifted to Sasaram. His temporary grave still exists on the small hillock known as Kalanjari towards the east of the fort.[25]

Islam Shah, his son, held it after that. He renamed it Sher Koh. After his death, the Baghela/Bundela forces recaptured it.

Akbar captured the fort in 1569 and gifted it to Birbal or Raja Mahesh Das.

Kalinjar Fort
Credit: Taha Ahmed

In 1688, the Bundela leader, Raja Chhatrasal, captured the fort. Chhatrasal was the father of the famous Mastani, who married Peshwa Baji Rao I. The British took the fort in 1812.

Forts were built for strategic and defensive purposes so, as was usual, this fort too is surrounded by ramparts with four gateways for access.

The Kalinjar fort situated on the top of the hill has two entrances, of which the principal one is on the northern side, towards the town, while the other is at the southeast angle leading towards Panna. The second gateway on the northern side has seven entrances which were approached by a flight of stone steps, which are now extant. Thankfully, now we can drive in from the other gateway, as the steps of the second gateway are extant only in the beginning of the pathway and are steep and at times difficult to ascend.

The first entrance/gateway is the Alam Darwaza, constructed during the reign of Aurangzeb Alamgir as indicated by an inscription fixed on the top of gate bearing the date AH 1084 (AD 1673), when it was made, as strong as the 'wall of Alexander'.

The others are Ganesh Darwaza (after an adorable statue of Lord Ganesha on it), the Chandi Darwaza or Chauburji Darwaza (the gate of the four towers), the Balkhandi Mahadeo Darwaza, which leads to a shrine of the same name situated around halfway down the hill. The other gateways are the Budhabhadra Darwaza named *Swargarohana* or 'ascent towards heaven' because it was built at the steepest point, the Hanuman Darwaza (after a statue of Lord Hanuman) and the Lal Darwaza (made from red sandstone), near the top of the ascent. The Bhairav Kund, with an enormous statue of Kal Bhairava carved in the rock lies to the west of this gateway.

The final gateway which leads into the fort is called Bara Darwaza.

We had entered from the motorable gateway and were greeted by a number of buildings from the medieval age. The most noteworthy among the secular structures (totalling 15) are the gateways and the palaces. The Rani Mahal, Rang Mahal, Aman Singh Palace and Chaube Mahal from the late-Mughal period are notable. Aman Singh was the great-grandson of Raja Chhatrasal.

There are 22 religious structures, which include temples, mosques and kunds.

The architecture, as was customary in the Bundela style of construction, is square, multistoreyed and built around a courtyard. There are chajja, overhanging balconies and chatris. There are rows of rooms with open terraces around the courtyard. Most of them are in a dilapidated state.

The Aman Singh Palace has been made into the site museum and has a treasure house of statues excavated from the fort that are now kept in the galleries around the open courtyard.

There's a very picturesque kund known as Koth Tirth with a flight of steps leading down to it, near the Aman Singh Palace. This was a holy kund, as many images of gods and goddesses were discovered here and there are pilgrims' inscriptions on it. It is also the largest at around 100 yards in length. These kunds were created by cutting the rocks to hold water.

Two other kunds of note are Sita Kund, a natural reservoir, and Pandu Kund, a circular basin. A deep well/reservoir called Patal Ganga is cut in the rocks. Another stunning kund is the Bhairav ka Jhirka with a colossal statue of

Mandukya Bhairav carved during the Bundela rule. This is in an area which is not easily accessible, but more on that later.

A small cave called Sita Sej, with a stone bed and pillow, was probably used by an ascetic. It has an inscription in characters from the eighth century on the entrance. It is situated beyond the Bara Darwaza, the main gateway of the fort.

The presence of mosques and a graveyard testify to Islam Shah and Akbar's occupation of the fort.

Three of the gateways to the township of Tarahati survive. The one on the north is known as the Kampta Gateway, the western gateway is known as the Panna Gateway and then there is the Rewa Gateway, which is situated in the northwestern part of Tarahati. The road which passes through it leads to the 'Sravan' statue and a number of tanks, before leading to the second important hill of the region known as Kalinjari or Chhoti Kalinjri. This 'Sravan' statue is carved on the rock face.

It was this area which is comparatively unexplored and which I was fortunate to explore.

On a trip to Kalinjar in August 2021, we set off with Samir Kher of Deep Dive India and Sanatkada Heritage to see this spectacular piece of art. Samir warned us that it was a difficult walk along the ramparts and that we would need to go outside the fort gates to see one of its outer walls. The walk was indeed tough but spectacular and we went out of the Panna and Rewa Gateway and to the road going down to the village. The Panna Gateway is in ruinous condition with broken stone steps which had to be negotiated carefully but the Rewa Gateway is well-preserved.

They lead to the township of Tarahati but instead of

going down towards it we climbed towards an area called Mandukya Bhairava. The difficulties of walking through ruinous walls with a sharp drop off the hill scarp, dense undergrowth, thanks to monsoons, was offset by the sheer joy of seeing this glorious sculpture. For those with an adventurous spirit I would advise visiting; it's difficult, but if approached cautiously, it is not dangerous or impossible. However, one should go in a group so that someone has your back. The rock-cut sculpture, amazing in its design and scope, is not something that has been viewed by many people. Bhairava as we all know is one of the incarnations of Lord Shiva and that's who we were going to see. But what or who was Mandukya? That's the name by which the Shiva sculpture is described in the inscriptions all around it on the rockface by pilgrims and devotees. It's a name used for a frog, though there's a deep reservoir there called Bhairav Jhirka which is too deep for frogs to survive. I emailed Mr Vijay Kumar, whose detailed article in the *Indian Journal of Archaeology*[26] on the inscriptions of Kalinjar told me about the name. He replied that a 'A plant called nirgundi also known as meudi grows in abundance in that area. I think this place is named after this weed.'

Finally, we had taken the turn and above me were again steep steps and the image we had come to see: a huge sculpture carved into the wall of Lord Shiva as the Gajantaka or Gajasurasamhara, which is an aggressive/destructive form of Shiva as a martial lord who killed an elephant demon. The story occurs in a couple of Puranas as well as some other sources. The killing was so violent that he skinned him and danced within his hide—which is why in some examples he dances on the elephant's head and lifts the hind legs up.

When a demon assumed the form of an elephant and terrorized Brahmins who were worshipping the linga, Shiva emerged from this linga, slew the demon and removed the elephant skin, thereafter wearing the hide on his upper body. This icon was popular in Pallava and Chola art, which portrayed him dancing vigorously in the flayed elephant hide of Gajasura. What makes the image in Kalinjar very special is that it is fifth-century Gupta Era, preceding the sculpture in Elephanta Caves which is of circa AD 550. The rock wall around it is carved with many images but none as exquisite as that of Parvati, sitting on a couch, supported by her arm on the wall at a right angle to the Gajantaka image.

On the way, we passed a stone chamber which enclosed a water reservoir named Mrigdhara, with carvings of deer inside and outside the stone enclosure. Inscriptions even give the names of the deer as Dina, Pandit, Vilochana, Mana, etc. The names of the deer are from the thirteenth–fourteenth century including inscription with a salutation to Neelkanth.[27]

These gateways and plans of the fort are captured for posterity in a series of pen and ink and watercolour drawings by Frederick Charles Maisey from an album of 60 drawings dated 1847–1854 and some by unknown artists.[28]

Some of the sculptures, like the one of Lord Ganesh and the churning of the ocean, are still well preserved and it's always a thrill to be able to compare past and present.

Another great contribution of Kalinjar seems to have been in the field of music, as the Baghela rulers were patrons of art and music. Nayak Bhakshu, credited with the creation of dhrupad, migrated to Kalinjar from Gwalior. From here, he went to the court of Sultan Bahadur Shah of Malwa on the latter's request.

Perhaps that accounts for the astounding acoustics. Askari Naqvi of Sanatkada Heritage sang a thumri for us in a pavilion built in the walls of the koti tirth baoli. It was quite a long distance away but the sound was crystal clear to us, sitting on the opposite end.

Along with this impregnable fort, the Chandela rulers also built the magnificent Khajuraho temples and the Ajaigarh Fort.

It is said that the sarovar over the Neelkanth temple contains treasures and there are indications written on its walls which can guide you. I don't know how true it is, for surely someone must have found it if it had been material treasure. To my mind, it is treasure of the spiritual kind, for I felt a great sense of peace there.

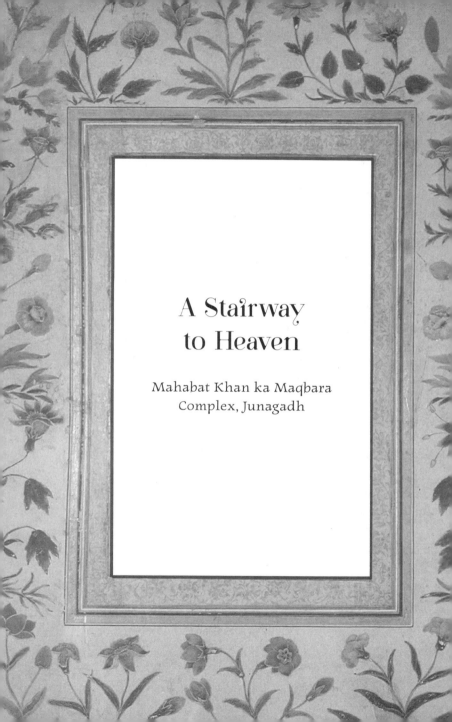

A Stairway to Heaven

Mahabat Khan ka Maqbara
Complex, Junagadh

The word Junagadh means Old Fort and this city is situated at the foothills of the Girnar Hills and has a long and sacred history.

This city was ruled by the Mauryans (319 BCE) and has many relics of the era, the most famous being the Girnar Rock Edict of Emperor Ashoka.

In 1822, Colonel James Tod stumbled upon an important piece of Indian history lying like a sleeping elephant beside the path leading up to Mount Girnar: the Girnar Rock Edict.

He described it as: 'a huge hemispherical mass of dark granite, which like a wart upon the body has protruded through the crust of mother earth, without fissure or inequality, and which by the aid of "iron pen", has been converted into a book.'

Todd had the writing on the edicts faithfully copied and sent to the great scholar James Prinsep in 1837. Prinsep decoded the Brahmi script, in which they were written, with an iron implement/pen. He also discovered and established that the Odisha rock edict and the Girnar edict were basically identical and helped establish Ashoka as a genuine historical figure.

The protective building around the edicts was built in 1900 by Nawab Rasool Khan of Junagadh which was repaired and restored in 1939 and 1941 by later rulers. It has now been housed in a lovely building.

The earliest inscriptions on the rock are from the third century BC (257 BC) with an edict of the Mauryan emperor Ashoka.

Like the elephant, this rock also had a long memory and carries an important message:

Junagarh Maqbara—Bahauddin Tomb

On each occasion one should honour another man's sect, for by doing so one increases the influence of one's own sect and benefits that of the other man; while by doing otherwise one diminishes the influence of one's own sect and harms the other man's. Again, whosoever honours his own sect or disparages that of another man, wholly out of devotion to his own, with a view to showing it in a favourable light, harms his own sect even more seriously. Therefore, concord is to be commanded, so that men may hear one another's principles and obey them.

The Buddhist caves in the Uparkot or Junagadh Fort are another reminder of the city's Buddhist past.

Junagadh was ruled by the Babi Muslim dynasty, established in 1735 by Sher Khan Babi. It became a British protectorate in 1807.

There was a dispute over the kingdom's accession to India as Nawab Mahabat Khanji III wanted to join Pakistan despite having no common boundary with it.

Under pressure from the Indian government and threat of military action by Sardar Vallabhbhai Patel, the Nawab fled to Pakistan and Junagadh was integrated with the Indian State in November 1947.

However, if you are a heritage lover like me, chances are that the minute you hear the name Junagadh you connect it to the magnificent Mahabat Khan maqbara or mausoleum.

The traditional cemetery of the Babis is located in the heart of the city, called Chitta Khana Chowk. When I was exploring Junagadh, I saw some black onion domes peeping from behind a boundary wall. I kept exploring the market area till I found a way inside. This was the old Babi family graveyard.

The entrance is small and has a big signage describing the place: the mausoleum of the first nawab, Sher Khanji (titled, Bahadur Khanji) and his wife. The mausoleum of Maiji Saheba is exquisite[29] but now gets so crowded that it has become difficult to access and not everyone can go there.

Other nawabs are buried here. Since this is a family cemetery, there are many graves—some simple, some elaborate with onion domes, great stone carvings and a sense of history and neglect. One can easily see that the design of the more famous maqbara of Mahabat Khan II and Bahauddin Khanji are present here.

The maqbara of Mahabat Khan stands right in the centre of the town, opposite the High Court and very close to the railway station.

There were three Muhammad Mahabat Khanji, who

were the nawabs of Junagadh. While the first nawab's rule (Muhammad Mahabat Khanji I ruled during 1758–1774) is not talked about, the other two are famous. Muhammad Mahabat Khanji II (r. 1851–1882) is famous for the maqbara he made for himself and is named after him. Muhammad Mahabat Khanji III fled to Pakistan after Junagadh was integrated with the Union of Indian states.

We are concerned here with the second Muhammad Mahabat Khanji who left behind an everlasting memory.

The construction of this maqbara was started in 1878 by Mahabat Khanji himself and was completed after his death by his successor Bahadur Khanji in 1892. Nawab Mahabat Khan II was an admirer of European architecture and used the Gothic style, very popular in Europe at the time, blended with Islamic architectural style.

Mahabat Khan II's mausoleum is crowned by a large onion dome and surrounded by a cluster of smaller onion domes. The facade is elaborately carved with decorative Gothic arches, columns and French windows.

The door to the tomb is locked and through the thick iron link doorway, I could see the dilapidated state of the graves and wooden door to the main grave chamber.

A photograph from 1900[30] shows a low rail around Mahabat Khan's maqbara but there were no traces of it when I visited in 2019. There was a wall which enclosed both the mausoleums and no individual wall.

Though everyone talks of Mahabat Khan ka Maqbara, it is his wazir or Prime Minister Bahauddinbhai Hasanbhai whose maqbara with its spiral staircase is more popular, and that is what drew me to Junagadh. Most people confuse the two. The famed maqbara that one sees in the brochures is of the prime minister of Mahabat Khan II, who was also known as Bahauddin Khan.

Bahauddin Khan built this maqbara during 1891–96, at an expense of ₹81,559.70 annas as described on the board there.

He also constructed the very magnificent Bahauddin College in the city and the nearby Jama Masjid. In fact, the keys to the mausoleum are with the imam of the Jama Masjid, who is also responsible for its upkeep.

I have seen many tombs all over India but this is the most uniquely designed of them all. It is a curious blend of European Gothic, Islamic and Indian architecture.

His mausoleum has one large onion dome, with two smaller ones adjoining it and exterior decorative flourishes. The doorway here is quite big with inscriptions on either side describing the construction. The fame of this mausoleum lies in the four minarets, each encircled from top to bottom with winding staircases on the outside. These give a unique effect as most minarets have internal spiral staircases. The Jama Masjid, also built by him, has the same external staircase in the minarets. The Jama Masjid has fared much better and is in very good condition, as it's a functioning mosque, than the tombs of the nawabs and his vizier, who built it. Its arcaded facade, minarets and cluster of onion domes are impressive.

Today, the maqbaras are a dark and dirty brown, but in a black-and-white photograph from 1895 one can see that the domes are of a much lighter colour.[31] The decorative elements are very clear on the gateway.

An inscription next to the entrance says that the income of the village of Jhalansar and part of the revenue from the village of Goladhar had been set aside for the upkeep of the two maqbaras and the adjoining mosque by the then present, Nawab Saheb Bahadur. The upkeep is now being done by the ASI.

The inscription adds that it was built under the supervision of Mir-e-Imarat, superintendent architect, Shaikh Mahmud Hafizuddin alias Mahmud Bhai, cousin of the Wazir Saheb.

As you enter the complex, a board by the Department of Archaeology, government of Gujarat, says it is protected under the Gujarat Ancient Monuments and Archaeological Sites and Remains Act, 1965 (Gujarat Act No. 65 of 1965). The usual warning follows, that anyone found defacing, destroying or removing any part of it or imperilling it in any manner will be liable to punishment with a fine up to ₹5,000, or imprisonment up to three months, or both. However, no one takes it seriously. When I went early in the morning, I saw a group of children playing cricket there. The monument is already compromised by plants and shoots of trees growing on it, forcing it to crack. I stood there aghast at the damage a cricket ball could do to the surface decoration of the mausoleum, but familiarity breeds contempt and no one seemed to care.

A wedding shoot was taking place but at least they were not harming it in any way.

It's a very popular location for pre-wedding shoots and I suppose at least someone cares for its looks even if it is only as a romantic background.

I had come to Junagadh with a lot of excitement to see these fabled mausoleums. I climbed to the top of the minaret via the spiral staircase, and though it was an achievement unlocked, I left with a very heavy heart because of the utter neglect and lack of care I had witnessed.

How long will these magnificent structures survive like this?

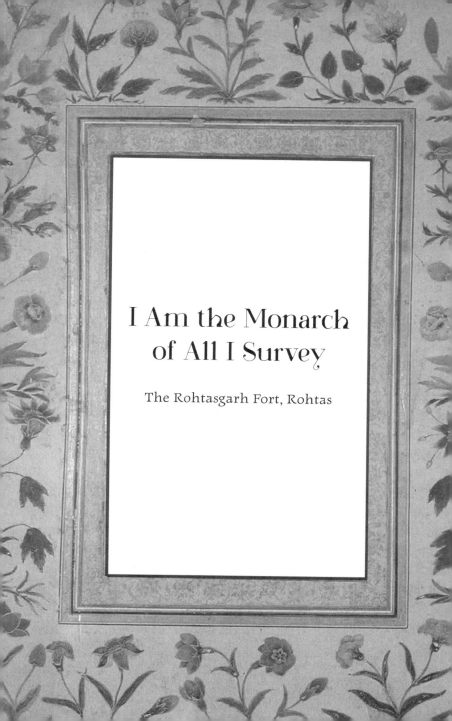

I Am the Monarch of All I Survey

The Rohtasgarh Fort, Rohtas

The state of Bihar is home to innumerable historical legacies. It was here that the city state of Magadha flourished. The first Indian empire of the Mauryas (322–185 BCE), with its capital in Pataliputra, had existed here. The Gupta empire (third century CE–543 CE) too had its capital in Pataliputra.

Two major religions, Buddhism and Jainism, originated here. It has been a place of historical, religious and cultural importance since days of antiquity.

The Buddhist shrines in Mahabodhi, Rajgir and Vaishali attract devotees and tourists from all over the world. It was in Mahabodhi, under the sacred Bodhi tree, that Lord Buddha had gained enlightenment.

Lord Mahavir, the twenty-fourth Jain Tirthankar, attained nirvana in Pawanpuri in the Nalanda district.

The Afghan ruler Sher Shah Suri is buried in a magnificent tomb in Sasaram.

These are all well-known destinations but my interest was the Rohtas Fort, which is rather difficult to reach because of hilly terrain and forests. However, not one to be deterred, I set off to visit it in a four-wheel drive and after some picturesque scenery and adventures along the way, managed to finally reach the place.

The Rohtas plateau, on which the fort is built at a height of 1,500 feet above sea level, is situated on the Kaimur Range above the river Sone. It rises sharply from the plains below. The locals and die-hard adventurers, of course, prefer to climb the steep face of the hill and climb the steps. These were beyond me, not because of the physical challenge alone, but also the time factor. The fort is situated on the Mirara ghat and its walls overlook the valley below.

Rohtas Fort

The steps lead up to the ancient Shiv Temple which is very popular among devotees. This temple is also linked with Rohitashva.

The way to the fort is an impressive sight with its lofty gates, a craggy surface, lakes, woods, pastures, meadows, arable and wood land. In places, the rocks have been cut by torrential rain and, at one point, our vehicle got stuck and had to be pushed to cross the sharp rocks.

As per legend, the hill on which the Rohtas Fort is situated was named in memory of Raja Harishchandra's son Rohitashva. Raja Harishchandra is mentioned in the Markandeya Purana and other religious texts. He gave away his kingdom and sold his family and himself into bondage to fulfil a vow he had made to the sage Vishwamitra.

In 1539, Sher Shah captured the area and built a fort on the southern side of the tableland. He named the fortress after himself—Shergarh—and his family lived here during his campaigns. The fortress commanded a view of utmost richness and magnificence.

To the east of the palace complex, is the mosque of Habash Khan and his mausoleum. He was an Abyssinian darogha in Sher Shah's reign, who oversaw the building of the fortifications during the Afghan's rule. The tomb building is 48 sq. feet six inches with an elevation of 65 feet. On the four corners of the compound, 96 sq. feet, there are four small hexagonal guardrooms one of which used to lead to a circular reservoir 54 feet in diameter and six-feet deep. This was maintained to water the palace and the garden. It is all in ruins now.

In 1562, Raja Bharmal Kachhwaha of Amer, a principality in Rajasthan met the Mughal emperor Akbar and thus, began a long association between the Kachhwaha clan and the Mughals. Raja Bharmal offered his daughter's hand in marriage to Emperor Akbar in exchange for the Badshah's backing to Bharmal's claim to the gaddi of Amer. The Kachhwahas went on to become one of the most powerful rulers of Rajasthan.

Raja Bharmal's grandson Raja Man Singh (1550–1614) became the highest ranking mansabdar of the Mughal court.

Emperor Akbar held him in high regard and gave him the title of Farzand (Persian for son) and was appointed to lead several important military campaigns.

In 1587, Raja Man Singh was the commander of the Mughal army that conquered the strategically-located fort of Rohtas making it his capital.

Once on top of the plateau, the visitor is greeted by an undulating land with village settlements, fields and, of course, ruins. Originally the area was very hilly with bare rocks visible and fine red soil, but years of habitation have tamed the rocks, at least on the way to the palace.

That rulers and soldiers of yore would have traversed these same roads adds to the sense of history and makes up for all the jerks and bumps of a dirt road, which at times is a challenge for the modern visitor.

It is quite a long drive up to the fort. The surrounding security walls are still standing overlooking the steep cliff on one side and though battered in places, are a testimony to the strength of the stone blocks used and the artisans' skills.

According to Montgomery Martin[32] the sides of the hill were very steep, almost perpendicular and the 84 passages (including the neck) in it were more or less fortified. It covered an area of 28 miles (45 kilometres). The vulnerable part of the fortress is indeed the neck, by which it is joined to the tableland called Kathautiya. A ditch was built here as a security measure. Man Singh also constructed two grand gateways on the way to the fort known as the Singh Darwaza and the Kathautiya.

The details of the gateways were described in Maulvi Muhammad Hanif Kuraishi's survey for the ASI,[33] 'The Singh Darwaza, inside the Kathautiya, derives its name from the figures of two lions inserted in the masonry of the huge rectangular bastions flanking the long and narrow flight of steps leading up to the gateway.' These were built on the eastern side by Raja Man Singh and were within 40 yards of each other to defend the neck of the plateau.

Though I entered through two gateways on the way to the fort and one into the boundary of the gate, I did not see any lions. The first gateway, which is the Kathautiya Darwaza where the tall imposing walls and bastions start, had a Persian inscription on top and roseate patterns on it. We passed through four such gateways before reaching the main palace and, of course, we stopped at all of them but the lions were missing on them. Either it has been ruined or I did not go on that route. The roads are dirt tracks and I had gone when pre-monsoon showers had caused flash floods so we just followed the straightest path to the fort. Even then, our four-wheel-drive vehicle got stuck in a rocky depression and it was only because of the skill of the driver and help from local villagers that our vehicle managed to cross it. I spent a considerable amount of time exploring the Kathautiya Darwaza, its battlements, bulwarks and other defensive measures, marvelling at the sheer drop below and the beautiful green of the tree-covered slopes through the musketry embrasures.

Over the arched entrance of the Kathautiya gateway is a Persian inscription of two lines and a Sanskrit one of eight lines, both in bold letters. The Sanskrit inscription is partly hidden by the branches of the trees around it but the Persian is clearly visible.

Kuraishi writes that the Sanskrit inscription is sadly damaged, but it seems to be very similar to that of the Hathiya Pol (Elephant Gate) of the palace.

The Persian inscription is also partly damaged and the dots indicate the damaged unreadable portions. It consists of three lines and reads as follows:

Line 1: ...Said, I have heard from the rider of the grey-horse of the world that... Raja Man Singh constructed a (fortification like the) China wall

Line 2 (Completed): During the *shiqdari* of Purohit Sridhar and Gopal Das, and under the supervision of Bahai Khan Bani Isra'il and Darogha Bal Bhadr.

Line 3: Wearer (or keeper) of the sacred thread, by the architect Ustad Mubarak. Written on the first of the month of Zil-q'ada in the year 1015 H. (=AD 1607).[34]

The other gateways mentioned by Kuraishi are the Lal Darwaza and Mendra Darwaza. He calls the latter the least pretentious of the four and we had passed through one that fit the bill. The Ghazi Darwaza, which commands the Ghora Ghat, is said to be the gateway through which Sher Shah Suri had entered the fort and that accounts for its name Ghazi, which means warrior. Since Kuraishi says that there are many tombs near it along with the tomb of Habash Khan, this must be the one we passed on our way.

On the way to the palace building are the ruins of a Jama Masjid built in AD 1543 during Sher Shah's reign. It is made of white sandstone and comprises three domes. The three-domed Jama Masjid is very typical of the mosques made in Sher Shah's reign. It is 40 feet in height, the diameter of the central dome is 24 feet and of those, on the two sides of it are 21 feet each. Today it stands desolate in the middle of fields and serves as an animal shelter. The mihrabs are sturdy and simple.

Along the way there is a mausoleum of perhaps Habash Khan, the darogha or the superintendent of works under Sher Shah.

Eventually, after a short stop at a water reservoir where children were diving in to beat the heat, we reached the outer gates of the palace complex. A walled enclosure with two gateways led us in. We stopped our car near the Hathiya Pol and walked in. Apart from this prominent gateway, we could see a few projecting balconies, typically Mughal in their design, decorating the facade at irregular intervals. This was picturesquely broken by isolated chatris and pavilions and the upper storeys of the Throne Room or Darbar Hall, making it an ideal subject for photography or as the current craze is, each chatri or pavilion is a perfect point for selfies.

Raja Man Singh was also appointed as governor of several key Mughal provinces. One of them was Rohtas in Bihar, which he chose as his capital.

Man Singh was a prolific builder and apart from the fort in his own principality of Amer, he built forts in the places he was posted to. According to Catherine Asher, this fort was the first introduction of courtly Mughal style of architecture to Eastern India.[35]

This was the largest non-imperial Mughal fortress and even in its desolate state today, the entrance gate is magnificent.

The Hathiya Pol, so called because of the carved elephants on either side of the gateway, leads into a vaulted space and then inside the fortress. On the inner gateway, there are two inscriptions in Sanskrit and Persian describing the completion of the fort.

The Persian inscription reads that the fort has been built primarily for Sultan Muhammad Jalaluddin Akbar Badshah Ghazi by his servant Man Singh, while the eight-line Sanskrit inscription describes Man Singh's role as head of the Kachhwaha clan, calls him king of kings and omits any reference to Akbar. In the Persian inscription, written on the 27th of Rajab 1005 AH (16 March 1597), the names of the priest Sridar, darogha Bal Bhadr and architect Ustad Mubarak are given.

Catherine Asher writes that this suggests he was aware of both his roles, as a Mughal mansabdar, a raja and head of the Kachhwaha clan.[36] This is further emphasized by the fort's resemblance to a Mughal fort.

There is a second Persian inscription from 1607 in the Rohtas Fort which is silent about Emperor Jahangir who was ruling then; neither does it extol the rank of Man Singh.

The palace was constructed on a north-south axis, with its entrance to the west with barracks for soldiers in front. The inner archway of the Hathiya Pol leads into an open court, of which the west side was originally occupied by a gallery providing a covered passage from the gateway to the building designated as 'office' or Baradari. It is a two-storeyed building. Today, with overgrowth, dirt and grime of neglect, it is difficult to make out much, but Kuraishi writes that the Baradari, which is perhaps the most symmetrically arranged part of the whole palace, is of a pleasing design.

The verandah has deep sloping eaves between two side walls with jharokhas and small doors. The verandah is supported on four sets of octagonal pillars to give it an elegant finish. There are two cupolas on the northeast and northwest corners of the roof. Kuraishi mentions eight pillars supporting it but since I could not climb on top of the roof I could only see the cupolas from below.[37]

Inside there is a huge central hall and rooms on the corners. A staircase leads up to the second level and roof.

An 1870 photograph by Joseph Beglar also shows these signs of neglect.[38] There are a series of photographs by Beglar on the British Library website which can be used to compare the condition of the monument over a century later.[39]

Following the few people who were there (mostly devotees who had come to the temple) we entered the public apartments. The first of these are called Eunuch's Quarters by Kuraishi and it leads to the Rang Mahal, which was used by Raja Man Singh as his sleeping quarters.

The irregular arrangement of the palace adds to a sense of magnificence, its sturdy architecture betraying the grandeur of its builder and overgrown grass in front of each apartment adding to the feeling of impermanence in a structure meant to be permanent.

The walls are constructed of square stone blocks placed in an irregular manner. The roofs consist of stone beams and flags covered with plaster. These would have originally been plastered and painted but are now scratched and are bare in most places. The buildings are built on multiple levels, going up to four storeys in the case of the throne room or Takht-e Badshahi building. We wandered through the darbar hall of Raja Man Singh and it must have been magnificent when in use. The lower portion was Raja Man Singh's residence and I have a feeling that the lower rooms of this building must have been very elegant.

The throne room is on the second level and is the most attractive room of the fort. It was connected to the Zanana Mahal across the roof of the three rooms, thus forming the north wing of the ground floor.

The remains of the vaulted arches in the side rooms, the pigments indicating presence of paintings, the parapets and balustrades, all speak in one voice of a grandeur that has disappeared with time.

Of special mention is Raja Man Singh's Shish Mahal (Mirror Palace), which is located in the middle of the fort. It is built on four levels with a cupola on top. This was used for residential purposes on the lower levels and assembly and entertainment on the upper levels. This was probably also used as a residence for the ladies, according to Kuraishi, probably the chief wife.

All around it, beyond the overgrown grass, are rows of rooms for the guards and retainers. A little way away from this garden and Shish Mahal is a long building designated Diwan-e-Aam or Nach Ghar.

As we wandered in and out of the rooms, we came to an elevated palace with a depression in the centre. From the map given by Kuraishi, this seems to be the Phul Mahal or Flower Palace. This depression was originally a cistern with a water jet. Now, it was filled with mud and someone had placed flowers in it, making for a very dramatic visual.

The ornamented walls and niches with floral designs, which probably gave it its name, were desperately trying to make their presence felt through the grime. This was perhaps the Diwan-e-Khas. A sense of loss and sadness crept in seeing it physically and imagining its past glory.

We walked out of the western opening of the palace complex towards the temples and the hanging room. On the way, we passed water bodies and come upon the most picturesque and sweeping view of the valley below; green as far as one can see.

The Ganesh Temple and the Jain Temple are a little walk away from the palace compound. The Ganesh Temple is built in the Rajasthani style. A pencil and wash drawing by Thomas and William Daniell of the temple shows it intact[40] as compared to the present when only the steeple remain and the outside mandaps are in a ruinous condition. The description by the Daniells says,

> This building, composed of grey granite, is of singular construction, and has the appearance of great antiquity. The Hindoos, who formerly preferred elevated places for their temples, could not, it would seem, resist the temptation of building in this place, the situation being delightful, and water and wood, with every other convenience abundant.[41]

To the west of the Ganesh Temple is a building that the locals call Hanging House. As per legend, a local faqir was thrown into the 1,500-feet-deep trench situated here but nothing happened to him. Eventually, he was buried alive.

In later years, this fort provided shelter to Prince Khurram, who later ascended the throne as Emperor Shah Jahan when he rebelled against his father Emperor Jahangir. It was here that Mumtaz Mahal gave birth to Prince Murad.

The British captured the fort after the Battle of Buxar in 1764 and used it as a prison. During the Revolt of 1857, Kunwar Singh's brother Amar Singh took shelter from the British forces here.

This fort has seen glory days and is a repository of a varied and great history. It can easily be restored.

Red Taj Mahal

The Roman Catholic
Cemetery of Agra

It sometimes seems to me that the incomparable Taj Mahal has unnecessarily become a standard of all tombs in India. Each monument is unique in itself and doesn't need to be compared; yet, the trend of comparison continues. The tomb of Shahnawaz Khan, son of Abdur Rahim Khan-e-Khanan in Burhanpur is called the Black Taj Mahal; Ibrahim Rauza, tomb of Ibrahim Adil Shah II in Bijapur is called the Taj Mahal of the Deccan. This time, to my horror, I discovered that the exquisite tomb of Itmad-ud-Daula in Agra is called the baby Taj! This last one was named so because it is made completely of marble and was possibly an inspiration with its beautiful inlay work.

So when I was told of a Red Taj Mahal in Agra, I was curious, not because of the comparison but because it was located in the Roman Catholic Cemetery of Agra and was built for a Dutchman by his wife. This seemed very intriguing to me.

Though Christianity came to India very early (first century CE) via Kerala, the Roman Catholic sect came only in the sixteenth century. The Jesuit fathers of Goa were invited by Emperor Akbar to Agra to participate in the religious discussions he was holding. When Akbar shifted from Fatehpur Sikri to Agra Fort, the Jesuits also shifted to Agra, where they were given imperial permission to build a church in 1599–1600, known today as Akbar's church. Later on, Emperor Jahangir gave them land to expand it. The area is now called Padri Tola after the priests.

Built in 1611, a small chapel had petitions to God tied to its door and window screens by the faithful, just as in dargahs.

This is the the Padre Santos Chapel and is a high and spacious vaulted building which once had pointed floral

Red Taj Mahal

decorations inside, according to E.A.H. Blunt. Today it is simple and elegant, whitewashed with red sandstone jaalis. There are tombs of the Jesuit fathers inside it, including Father Marc Antoine Santucci, an Italian. 'Padre Santos Chapel' is possibly a corruption of Padre Santucci. It is known today as Marty's Chapel after Mortenepus (perhaps an Armenian priest), for his tomb is the oldest and most conspicuous tomb inside the chapel. The inscription is in Persian and refers to him as Khwaja Mortenepus, a servant of Jesus Christ.[42]

The cemetery was originally built for the Armenian Christians who came during the reign of Emperor Akbar (1556–1605) and the oldest grave belongs to John Mildenhall, an Englishman who had even had an interview with Emperor Akbar. He died in 1614 and was buried here. Mildenhall's tomb is probably the oldest English tomb in India. Blunt writes that 'the land for the cemetery was bought between 1605 and 1611 by Padre Joseph [da Costa], and made rent free by Jahangir in 1624.'[43]

Mildenhall's story is very interesting. He was a merchant who came to India to the court of the Mughals with a commendatory letter as a traveller by Queen Elizabeth I and gained a false reputation of being her ambassador to the court of the great Mughals![44]

The famous Walter Reinhardt 'Sombre' is also buried here. It is not certain how he got the name of 'Sombre.' One statement is that it was due to his swarthy complexion; another is that he had a sombre disposition, but whatever the reason, it got distorted to Samru.

That's how his wife came to be known as Begum Samru and is the more famous of the two. Reinhardt was a German mercenary who rose to become the the governor of Agra and ruler of a principality in present-day UP, called Sardhana. He married a Kashmiri dancing girl who ruled it after his death and is immortalized as Begum Samru. They moved to Agra after the marriage, and it was in Akbar's church that she converted to Christianity and was baptized.

Sombre died in Agra on 4 May 1778. He was buried in the Agra churchyard by his widow Begum Samru. His gravestone gives the date in a Persian chronogram. The tomb is simple and elegant: an octagonal shape with a dome in the Mughal style, and there are two graves inside. The other grave is that of Paul Frederic, killed in battle in October 1792.

Outside Samru's tomb is a sandstone pillar marking the graves of four children of a General Cuillier-Perron, who had served under Mahadji Scindia.

However, it is Hessing's tomb which is the most famous,

known locally as the Red Taj Mahal.

Colonel John William Hessing was born in Utrecht in 1739 and came to India as a 24 year old in 1763 and served under several masters. He served under the nizam of Hyderabad and later in 1784, joined the army of the Maratha chieftain, Mahadji Scindia. He fought many battles for Scindia and gained a good reputation.

He was eventually given the command of the first two battalions of the newly-raised Scindia army. After the death of Mahadji Scindia in 1793, he continued under Daulat Rao Scindia.

When ill health prevented active service, he was made the qiledar or commandant of Agra Fort by Scindia. He died in 1803 and was buried in the Roman Catholic cemetery which is in Nehru Nagar, Agra.

The red dome can be seen from afar and I entered the wooden gate with excitement. Right in front, towards the right of the entrance, was this beautiful red sandstone tomb. Of course it is not like the Taj Mahal but as it is domed, with vaulted doorways and built in the Mughal style of architecture and is in Agra, comparisons are inevitable. The square platform on which it stands is 11.25 feet high and 58 feet wide. Twin stairways, measuring 22 feet by 8.75 feet, lead up to the platform from the western side of the platform.

It has four slender minarets attached to the main tomb, its cupolas crowned by pinnacles. The square tomb in the middle of the platform measures 34.75 feet and is 28.5 feet high and has inverted lotus and finial blooms in the middle. The entrance is vaulted, very much in the Mughal style, with marble plaques above the door having a chronogram of the Colonel's date of death in Persian.

An octagonal chabutra is attached to the platform on all four corners. There is a fine carved panel running on the edge at the top and around the drum of the dome.

As in Mughal tombs, the actual grave is underneath and there were many other graves in the corridor outside the crypt. The square cenotaph chamber on top of the platform measures 17.75 feet.

This was built by his wife Anne Hessing at a cost of one lakh rupees.

The inscription on the grave, which was inscribed by Phillip Huniset, is fairly long, giving details of his life and service and reads:

John William Hessing, late a Colonel in the service of Maharaja Dawlut Row Sindiah, who, after sustaining a lingering and very painful illness for many years with true Christian fortitude and resignation, departed this life, 21 July 1803, aged 63 years, 11 months and 5 days. As tribute of their affection and regard this monument is erected to his beloved memory by his disconsolate widow, Anne Hessing, and afflicted sons and daughters, George William Hessing, Thomas William Hessing and Magdalene Sutherland. He was a native of Utrecht in Holland and came out to Ceylon in the military service of the VOC (Dutch East India Company) in the year 1752, and was present at the taking of Candia by their troops. Five years afterwards he returned to Holland and came out again to India in 1733, and served under the Nizam of the Deccan. In the year 1784, he entered into the service of Madarow Sindiah and was engaged in the several battles that led to the aggrandizement of that Chief and wherein he signalized himself so by his bravery as to gain the esteem and approbation of his employer, more particularly at the battle of Bhondagown near Agra in the year 1787, which took place between this Chief and Navab Ishmael Beg, when he then became a Captain, and was severely wounded. On the death of Madarow Sindiah in 1793, he continued under his successor, Dawlut Row Sindiah, and in 1798 he attained to the rank of Colonel and immediately after to the command of the Fort and City of Agra, which he held to his death.

According to F.S. Growse, in his book *Mathura: A District Memoir*, a French traveller Victor Jacquemont, who visited Agra in 1829–30, said that the 'Taj though pretty was hardly elegant and that the only pure specimen of Oriental architecture was the tomb of John Hessing in the catholic cemetery.'[45] There is no doubt that it was at this time that the Taj Mahal had fallen into disrepair and must have been overgrown with trees and not the way as it is today, which was mainly due to the efforts of Lord Curzon at the turn of the twentieth century, but I agree with Growse that his views are 'warped'.

Hessing's tomb is definitely elegant but can't be compared to the Taj Mahal, even on its worst day, as a specimen of oriental architecture.

Fanny Parkes in her journals, *Begum, Thugs and White Mughals* edited by William Dalrymple, describes it as a, 'beautiful mausoleum is the Catholic burial ground at Agra and is well worth a visit.'

She goes on to say that it was built by a 'native architect, by name Lateef, in imitation of the ancient Mohammedan tombs. The tomb is beautiful, very beautiful and in excellent taste.'[46]

Lateef, it seems, was an expert *parchinkar* who used to inlay marble with precious stones as well as draw pictures of the Taj Mahal and other monuments in Agra. She bought a few of them.

The cemetery itself is very well kept, is green and has a prevailing sense of peace. Not many people know of it and so I found no visitors there. The caretakers were very cooperative and took me around.

As I wandered around the cemetery, what struck me was the amalgamation of cultures. There was a grave with Allah and the sign of the cross both carved on it and many graves had Latin, English and Persian inscriptions on them.

∞

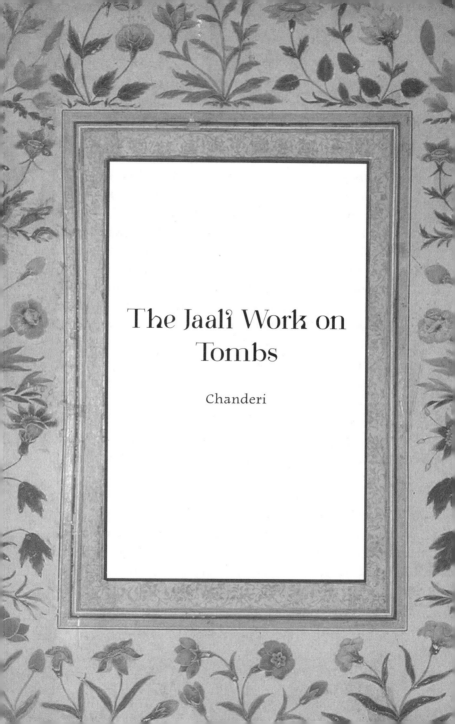

The Jaali Work on Tombs

Chanderi

Chances are you have heard of Chanderi in connection to the traditional textile craft that the town in MP is famous for. At least I knew only of Chanderi sarees.

Little did I know that this city, tucked away in the hills on the edge of Bundelkhand and Malwa, had such a great historical past. As per legend, it finds mention in the Mahabharata. It was ruled at various points by the Gurjara Pratihars (who first made it their capital), Bundela Rajputs, Delhi and Malwa Sultans, as well as the Mughals, Scindias and the British. It was on the trade routes and thus an important location. Having been a part of some very vibrant kingdoms with enthusiastic builders, especially the Malwa Sultans, Chanderi had surprises in store at every corner. It hid many gems such as Jain and Hindu temples, huge rock sculptures, *baolis*, tombs, chatris, madrasas and dargahs.

In fact, Abul Fazl in *Ain-i-Akbari* mentions that Chanderi had 14,000 stone houses, 384 markets, 360 caravan *sarais* and 1,200 baolis.

I visited most of the famous monuments including the fort, the mosques, temples, chatris, baolis and a huge rock-cut sculpture of the Jain tirthankara, Adinath, but it was a simple graveyard that held me spellbound.

The Malwa governor declared independence in the fourteenth century when the Tughlaq rule in Delhi was on the decline. Building activity was suspended in Delhi and artisans and skilled labour found generous patrons in Malwa where the kings were starting their construction activities. This, combined with Persian influence, gave rise to a Malwa style of architecture.

In Chanderi, according to Percy Brown, this was further supplemented by workmen evidently recruited from Ahmedabad.

Gujarat is famous for its stone latticework with the one on Sidi Saiyyed Mosque being world famous. The workmen of Gujarat, pioneers in translating wooden jaalis into stone, brought this characteristic skill with them, seeing as Tughlaq architecture was solid but hardly very ornamental.

It is these perforated stone screens, with their wonderful symbols, that epitomized Chanderi town for me. Jaalis serve not only as ornamentation but they also serve as windows, allow privacy and provide light and air.

Jaalis were used in India for temples and the word itself comes from Sanskrit and means a pierced screen. It is a common word in Hindi and Urdu for screens and nets. There is a separate chapter on jaalis in *Kāśyapā-Śilpā* (c. 1450) and *Śilpā-Ratnam* (c. 1600) called 'Jalaka-Laksanam', showing that the wooden jaali was introduced in stone in the early medieval period.

In a supplement to his book *History of Mughal Architecture*, R. Nath explains six types of jaalis prevalent in temple architecture according to their shape and design: the first two are titles for the forms of jaalis, the word *gonetrā* for semicircular and triangular-pierced screens and *hastinetrā* for square and rectangular shaped ones. The remaining four types are related to patterns for lattices, respectively called *nandyvartaā* swastika-based (incorrectly called interlaced by Nath); *Rjukriyam* or straight line geometrical designs; *Puspakarnā*, floral designs; and *Karnaā*, curvilinear patterns (confusingly referred as 'geometrical designs made of curved lines, precisely arabesques').[47]

A Saint, a Folk Tale and Other Stories

Chanderi

The happy marriage of arabesque and geometrical patterns to existing Hindu motifs and symbols such as the swastika, padma (lotus), chakra (circle), kirttimukha (glorious face), torana (free-standing ornamental or arched gateway), satkona (six-sided star), vyala (composite animal), makara (crocodile), sardola (composite animal), hastin (elephant) and mayurah (peacock) shows how 'extraneous inspirations were accepted and absorbed with the indigenous art in the evolutionary process and the style grew and developed under the liberal patronage of the Mughals.'[48]

Of course I did all this research later, as at that time I was just eager to soak in the beautiful architectural heritage of Chanderi.

My first stop was at the Bala-Qila, or fortress of Chanderi, which sits on a low flat-topped hill on the edge of the tableland overlooking the valley of the river Betwa. The fort is ruined but the carvings on the Khilji era mosque and the memorial erected to the legendary singer Baiju Bawra are worth visiting. The Qila is pretty lonely and I was the only person exploring it with my guide. Do remember to take a guide with you if you are alone.

The city is full of treasures and I had a beautiful time exploring them.

Driving into the town, I saw a board that read Hazrat Nizamuddin *parisar*. There were some old town houses with people living in them but that was not what I was looking for. I had read of a beautiful grave complex here. A young boy who saw us wandering asked us what we were looking for and led us through some passages in the houses to what he called the qabristan, or cemetery, in the inner city.

Inside the narrow lane, tucked between houses, were

some of the most exquisite stone lattice screens abounding with every kind of curvilinear and geometrical patterns on it.

Part of the wall of the complex is the mihrab wall of one of the tombs and it was breathtaking. As we entered, we were spellbound.

Though very neat and clean, the graves had no flowers or lamps on them. Most of the intricately-carved grave cenotaphs were under the open sky but a few were within domed tombs and square walls. The dome of one particularly beautiful grave had fallen down and the jaali was worse for the wear. The jaalis had obviously seen better days and are guarding the last sleep of the souls buried there. Their sleep is eternal and the jaalis are trying valiantly to keep pace for as long as they can.

According to the ASI board there, these are the graves of the family of the famous Delhi Chisti Sufi saint Hazrat Nizamuddin Auliya's descendants who had come to Chanderi. Since the Delhi nizami family does not have any record of anyone from their family moving here, I continued my research. I finally found it in an article by Simon Digby who describes that Hazrat Nizamuddin Auliya appointed Shaikh Wajh al-Din Yusuf as his *khalifa* and sent him to Chanderi in his lifetime.[49] The Shaikh however, would not accept anyone directly as his disciple during his master's lifetime and would initiate his disciples in front of a garment worn by Hazrat Nizamuddin Auliya. It is probably because of this that the graveyard is named after Hazrat Nizamuddin Auliya. It would have originally been the shaikh's *khanqah*. This is reinforced by Richard Eaton,[50] who writes that 'during Qutb al-Din Mubarak Khalaji's reign, for example, the shaikh [Hazrat Nizamuddin Auliya] sent his disciple Maulana Yusuf down to Chanderi.'

However, what I could research were some of the symbols such as the eternal knots, *nagabandhana,* which were carved on the stones, and were magical even in their broken state. The eternal knot symbolizing the interweaving of the spiritual path and flow of time and movement—cycle of life and death—seemed very appropriate here. Many of the symbols present on these jaalis are similar to the *kolam* and Rangoli patterns. My travels enrich me by teaching me the interconnection that almost everything in our wonderful country has with one another.

Digby writes further that these jaalis would date to around 1400 CE, or possibly earlier, and bear the influence of contemporary Mamluk craftsmen of Syria and Egypt.

The nearby Badal Mahal Gateway is again an imposing structure against the Chanderi Fort, with an exquisite arched jaali on its upper half. It is an isolated gateway and there is no Badal Mahal nearby but such majestic gateways are common in Chanderi. They were probably erected to commemorate certain important events. The 50-feet high Badal Mahal gateway is a double-arched entrance with circular and tapering bastions on the sides.

I found another such gateway, similar in design, in the middle of the village. It is called Madrasa ka Darwaza and maybe there was some madrasa here at one point of time.

Another beautiful compound is the Shaikhon ka Maqbara which is outside the city. They were *shahikhzadas* of the 18 Sufi families who came and settled in Chanderi. This one is totally desolate and one only sees an occasional goat herd but is haunting in its beauty and piety. Once again, simple tombs with delicate jaalis could be seen here.

One tomb, a simple domed structure, was painted green

and the grave inside was revered by the locals. It had a green cloth covering it and the scent of incense hanging over it. I too entered and recited the fatiha for the soul's deliverance.

Chanderi is a city of plenty for any lover of heritage. In the middle of the fields, we came across the Bada Madrasa. Though madrasa means school, this is actually a maqbara of the teachers in the madrasa. The ruins of the madrasa can be seen nearby.

It can be dated to the fifteenth century, when the Malwa Sultanate was ruling Chanderi. From afar, the tomb looks very unprepossessing. It is in a ruinous state and its dome had fallen a few centuries ago. But don't get taken in by its external appearance. Please do go in, for the jaalis around the grave enclosure are exquisite. These employ geometric, combination of geometric and curvilinear and complete curvilinear, such as medallion designs.

We have the eternal knot, the six-sided star and roundels with beautifully carved flowers decorating the walls.

It is a sandstone structure with an arched corridor surrounding the main grave compartment. This chamber is accessed by a single entrance door. The two graves inside are covered by the unusual and exotic carved black stone cenotaph with geometrical patterns in high relief.

The mihrab indicating the direction of Mecca for the faithful to face during prayers is opposite the entrance door.

Those who make and love rangoli/kolam will find much to inspire them here. I walked around in the corridor for a long time soaking in the devotion of the hands that had carved these intricate designs.

Our next stop was the Lakshman temple in the middle of the Parmeshwar pond. The pond is surrounded by chatris of Rajput rulers, poignant in their desolation and lofty ruins.

Nearby is the Shahzadi ka Maqbara. The way to the maqbara is paved with sati memorials of women who must have committed sati on their husband's funeral pyres and are tragically mute.

The maqbara itself stands on a 12-feet-high platform and has two storeys divided externally by a series of arched depressions and a projecting decorated eave. The eave is supported by beautifully carved serpentine brackets.

The division is uneven and the lower level is much taller. It has five closed arched walls in each direction. Traces of coloured tiles, which must have adorned it once, can be seen on the upper level. The dome, which must have been huge going by the monument, has fallen down and the Princess sleeps exposed to the elements.

It is called the Shahzadi ka Maqbara or princess's mausoleum as it is believed she was the governor's daughter. It is dated to 1420–35 CE. The cenotaph chamber is a single square room and has a single storey. The outside division is for strength and decoration.

Locals attribute a tragic love story to the princess in the best traditions of Romeo and Juliet and Laila and Majnu. The princess loved the commander of her father's army, but since her father was against it, he sent the army out to battle with instructions that the commander shouldn't return alive. He was fatally injured, but before dying, he managed to make his way to the spot where the mausoleum stands. When the princess found out, she came there and gave up her life to join him in the afterlife. A grieving father erected this memorial for his daughter.

Apart from the tombs, there are some other beautiful

destinations in Chanderi. It was once a very popular centre of Jain religion and the Khandagiri temples and rock-cut caves are a place of pilgrimage. The huge 45-feet high Lord Rishabhnath statue cut on a rock is breathtaking and inspires piety.

Before leaving Chanderi, one must visit its most impressive building, the Koshak Mahal. According to *Tarikh-e-Firishta* it was built in 1445 CE by the sultan of Malwa, Mahmud Shah Khilji, to commemorate his victory over Sultan Mahmud Sharqi of Jaunpur in a battle at Kalpi. Kalpi had been a bone of contention between the sultans of Jaunpur and Malwa which resulted in a battle between the two with the Malwa sultan gaining victory and control over Kalpi. Originally, it is said to have been seven storeys, but now only three remain.

They are four separate palaces in the shape of a cross, with a wide open passage in the middle: the two east-west and north-south bisect each other at right angles. All the four palaces are of equal dimensions, standing at equal distance from one another on the sides of passages which connect them as much as they separate them. It allows each part to stand independently and draw its ventilation and light freely on all the four sides and yet be interconnected through the overhead covered corridors. There are chatris in the middle of the wall, on each of the four corners.

It's a fascinating monument and though one can only walk in the middle, the arches and the play of light on them are breathtaking.

It is built of white local sandstone and the arches and doorways are decorated with roundels and brackets.

I visited two baolis; one was in the middle of nowhere,

quite a walk from the main road but worth the effort. I also visited a set of three chatris called Hanson ka Madia and, of course, the shops selling the famous Chanderi sarees and fabric.

Chanderi, though off the beaten track, deserves to be visited and become a mainstream tourist attraction for its architectural heritage.

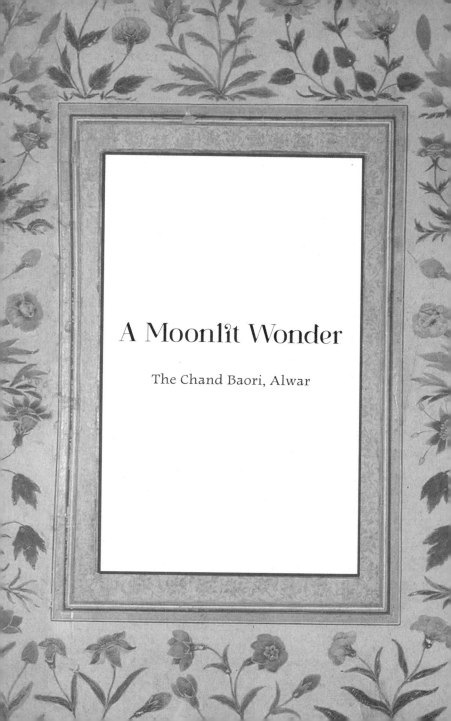

A Moonlit Wonder

The Chand Baori, Alwar

Whenever we think of Indian architecture, we think of the Taj Mahal, the Khajuraho temples, etc., but one of the most important contributions of Indian architecture is not its majestic forts, beautiful tombs and sublime temples and mosques but a unique water management system known as India's stepwells.

Water harvesting, storage and conservation systems have been found in the cities of the Indus Valley Civilization and we see them in the cities of Dholavira with its water reservoirs.

Delhi has many stepwells that are now just tourist spots, but at one time were the focus of the residents' lives.

The states of Gujarat and Rajasthan are normally dry with low rainfall and thus rainwater harvesting and conservation of water was of utmost importance, especially in periods of drought. Water has always played a major role in the lives of Indians with the rivers being worshipped as goddesses and it was just a natural corollary that the places where people gathered to worship, bathe or collect water for their daily needs became a focal point of their lives too.

The steps and platforms built on the banks of rivers known as ghats may perhaps have been the inspiration for the baolis/*baori*/*vav* as stepwells are called in Rajasthan and Gujarat. These also have places of worship and rooms for relaxation attached to it.

'The baori were generally structured with several stories let down steps to the bottom. Sometimes the complex engineering of Hindu and Islamic architecture made them stylish and unique. The Islamic version offers the arched side-niches while the Hindu architecture is full of decorative columns and pillars. Some of the bawdi are the fusion of Indo-Islamic culture,' writes Dr Anjali Pandey.[51]

The way a stepwell works is that there is a central, vertical shaft with water, which spreads out to a pool with a broad mouth and steps are built around it. The baoli itself can be round, rectangular or square and built with the simplicity or magnificence, depending on the means, at the command of the builder. The number of subterranean passages and rooms all around it would also depend on the same.

Its depth would depend on the underground water levels and thus inspire elaborate designs for the steps.

These were the precursors of exclusive clubs in ancient and medieval India where people could hang out with each other, provide hospitality to guests from out of town and also get water for their daily needs.

This water management system was discouraged by the British, who couldn't digest that the same water could be used for drinking as well as washing and bathing. They already had their own exclusive clubs and smoke rooms, so they just developed the systems of pumps and pipes thus leading to the drying up, clogging and eventual deterioration of this ancient lifestyle.

Though North India has many baolis, with Delhi alone boasting of about 30, some of which are still functional, my heart was enchanted by the one in Abhaneri. Just 200 kilometres from Delhi, it is one of the world's oldest, deepest and most spectacular stepwell. It is a long drive from Delhi, and from Jaipur it is 95 kilometres. We stayed in Alwar and had to drive 75 kilometres to reach it. On the way, one sees the occasional fort perched on top of a hill and the colours and hues of Rajasthan but the reward at the end is enchanting.

Called Chand Baori of Abhaneri, in Dausa district of Rajasthan, it is a feat of mathematical perfection from an ancient time. It has 3,500 steps built on 13 levels with 30 metre depth and with the most amazing symmetry as they taper down to meet the water pool. Said to be the upside-down pyramids, this baori was built somewhere between eighth and ninth century by Raja Chanda, a Rajput ruler.

It was attached to the temple of Harshat Mata, and it was a ritual to wash hands and feet at the well before visiting the adjoining temple.

The temple was razed during the tenth century but its remains still boast architectural and sculptural styles of ancient India. Harshat Mata is considered to be the goddess of joy and happiness. According to myth, the goddess is always cheerful, and she imparts her joy and happiness to the whole village.

Nowadays, there are railings and so we can't go down the steps but the temperature at the bottom is five to six degrees cooler and must have provided solace during the hot summer days and nights to the locals.

The Mughals added galleries and a compound wall around the well and today these house the remains of profuse and exquisite carving, which were either in the temple or in the various rooms of the baoli itself.

It is one of the few stepwells or rather step pond as Morna Livingston writes in *Steps to Water: The Ancient Stepwells of India* and it showcases 'two classical periods of water building in a single setting'.[52]

An upper palace building was added to one side of the baoli which can be seen from the trabeate arches used by the Chauhan rulers and the cusped arches used by the Mughals.

Access to these rooms is now blocked for tourists and as much as I wanted to, I couldn't go in and had to rely on my imagination.

Adina Mosque

Daulatabad Fort

Khusrau Bagh
Credit: Amit Pasricha

Sheikh Chehli Tomb

According to Livingston, 'The simplicity and brevity of the column shafts are attractive, and the pavilions they enclose are dark, simple and well-proportionated. In the Muslim portion of the well, however, the columns are carved in an unidentified hard green stone. The palace features more curves and organic shapes, in contrast to the straight lines found beneath it.[53]

Livingston also points out the spatial compactness of the stair triangles that run parallel to the stepwell's edge. 'The rise-to-run for each flight adds no more than 18 inches [45 centimetre] of width to eight feet [2.4 metre] drop, making an extremely sharp descent. The wall is so steep that the top of the stair triangles, seen from the pond's brim, alternately hide and reveal the people going down from above.'[54]

If the stones could speak, they would recount stories of a time when royalty sat in these rooms and heard the pitter-patter of the raindrops on the roof and see it splashing on the beautiful steps with strains of raag Malhar being sung by the court musicians.

Perhaps peacocks danced on the surrounding walls while court dancers danced with abandon on the platforms in front of the royal apartments.

Though now stripped of plaster, these stone walls must have been plastered with profuse paintings to emphasize the feeling of being in a beautiful moonlit oasis of happiness. The chanting of the priests as they went down to pray must have accentuated the spirituality of the shimmering water pool, and the singing of the women as they went to collect water must have gladdened even the hardest of hearts.

On three sides of the baori are galleries, which are now used as a museum to house the idols recovered from the well. Having visited Rani ka Vav in Patan, Gujarat, and having seen the beautiful carved sculptures on each level, I can well imagine that there must have been many sculptures all over the baori. Some of the sculptures adorn museums around the world. Two niche shrines at the beginning of the pavilions in the baori have a glorious carving of Goddess Durga in her Mahishamardini image and of Lord Ganesha.

I can't describe the absolute feelings of awe and wonder that descended on me as I stood there soaking in the ambience of the moonlit baori under the bright rays of the sun.

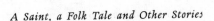

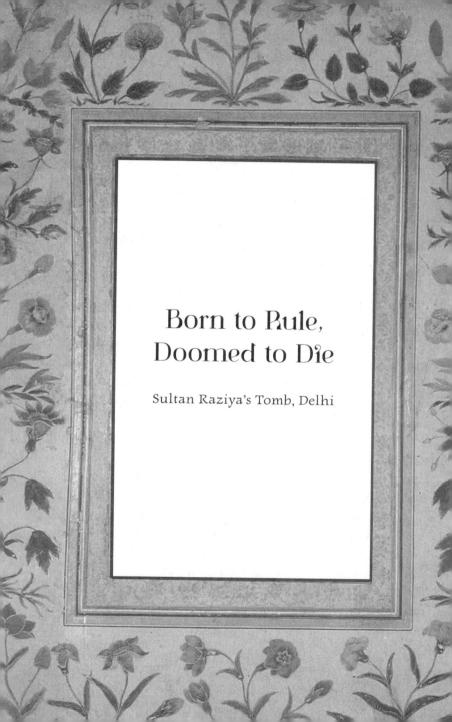

Born to Rule, Doomed to Die

Sultan Raziya's Tomb, Delhi

For several months, her face was veiled
—her sword's ray flashed, lightning-like, from behind the
screen.
Since the sword remained in the sheath,
many rebellions were left unchecked.
With a royal blow, she tore away the veil;
she showed her face's sun from behind the screen.
The lioness showed so much force
that brave men bent low before her.[55]

—Amir Khusrau

Delhi is one of the most visited cities of India and sees multitudes of tourists—foreign and domestic—every year. They visit the Red Fort, the Qutub Complex, the Humayun's Tomb and a few other famous places. But my favourite place lies hidden inside Old Delhi, away from the beaten track.

In the narrow lanes of Old Delhi, near Turkman Gate, is the grave of Delhi's only female monarch. Its approach is difficult to find, hidden as it is by shops and houses.

After entering from Turkman Gate and traversing the narrow lanes of Bhojala Pahadi till Bulbuli Khana, one comes upon a stone plaque put up by the ASI marking it as Sultan Raziya's grave.

Inside there are two stone graves, popularly known as Rajji Sajji (Raziya and Shazia). The identity of the second grave is unknown, but since Shazia rhymes with Raziya it must have caught the popular imagination.

It is possible that she was a loyal attendant or some relative. It is one of the romantic stories attached to her name now.

A small mosque in which prayers are held is well-maintained. The Imam lives in a porta cabin next to the graves.

Here lies one who has the distinction of being South Asia's first female monarch. Her father was Iltutmish the Third and the most famous Mamluk ruler of the Delhi Sultanate. Raziya was born of Iltutmish's favourite wife, Terken Khatoon, probably the daughter of Qutbuddin Aibak, as we do know that Iltutmish was his son-in-law. The graves are of simple stone on a plinth in a very restricted compound. But Raziya's legacy isn't simple nor should it be restricted; so let us examine that before coming to the question of her grave.

Iltutmish's eldest and most capable son was Nasiruddin Mahmud, whom he had groomed to be his successor. Unfortunately, he was killed in a battle in Lakhnauti, Bengal, where he was the governor in 1229 and his remaining brothers were considered incapable by the father of becoming the Sultan. Iltutmish had trained Raziya in politics and warfare from childhood and she was his favoured child, whom he appointed as his successor. When Iltutmish went on a campaign to Gwalior, he left Raziya in charge of the kingdom. He is said to have compared her worth to that of 20 sons.

When the nobles protested, Minhaj-us-Siraj, a thirteenth-century historian reports that Iltutmish replied, 'Engrossed in the pleasures of youth, none of them possesses the capability of managing the affairs of the country,'[56] whereas Raziya, his daughter, was the most worthy, as would be proven after his death.

This was a radical step for those days, when women

were confined to the harem alone. But Iltutmish, who was a far-sighted visionary, had not taken into account the aversion that the nobles had of being ruled by a woman. During the Mamluk reign, there was a band of very powerful noblemen (*Chihilgani*) who had removed Aram Shah, Aibak's son and put Iltutmish on the throne.

These nobles put Ruknuddin Firoz, (April 1236–October 1236) his younger son, on the throne. Ruknuddin was a young man given to the pursuit of pleasure and the reigns of the kingdom were in the hands of his mother Shah Turkan, an ambitious lady. One of her first steps was to try and isolate Raziya from the day-to-day work of the kingdom. She also had Raziya's youngest brother Muizuddin murdered. She used her new-found status to settle old scores and attempted to have Raziya murdered. Ruknuddin had gone out of Delhi for a battle and before he could return,

> The people of the city, upon this, rose, and attacked the royal kasr [castle], and seized the mother of Rukn-ud-Din, Firuz Shah. When Rukn-ud-Din, Firuz Shah, reached the city, insurrection had [already] broken out therein, and his mother had been made prisoner. The centre contingents [of the Dihli forces] and the Turk Amirs all entered Dihli and joined Sultan Raziyyat, pledged their allegiance to her, and placed her on the throne.[57]

Khwaja Abdullah Malik Isami in his *Futuh-us-Salatin* (1349–50) writes that

> she let loose her scarf from the window [of the royal palace] and said, 'Here I am, the daughter of His

Majesty; the royal crown befits my head. It is I whom the king had chosen as his heir-apparent; to me he had entrusted his seal.' She goes on to say, 'Should I acquit myself as a ruler better than man, you might keep me on the throne. Should you yourselves see things otherwise you may remove the crown from my head and give it to whomsoever you please and pay your homage accordingly.'[58]

By the time her brother came back to the city, Raziya's enthronement was complete and Shah Turkan had been thrown into prison. Both mother and son were executed on 9 November 1236.

This was the first time in the history of the Delhi Sultanate that the people of Delhi had decided a succession issue on their own initiative.[59] They were the main source of Raziya's strength. So long as she did not move out of Delhi, no rising against her could succeed and no palace revolution against her was possible. She was a monarch and she called herself Sultan Raziya, not Raziya Sultan which would be used for a daughter or a consort.

She titled herself Sultan Razat-al-Dunya wal-Din bint al-Sultan and Sultan Jalalat-al-Dunya wal-Din and struck coins in that name.

She ruled wisely for three years and six months (1236–1240). In the middle of her reign, she shrugged off her feminine dresses and donned the robes, tunic and turban of a man and according to Ibn Batuta (quoted by Eraly), 'She rode on horseback as men ride, armed with a bow and quiver, and surrounded with courtiers. She did not veil her face.'[60]

Patriarchy is not a new phenomenon and Minhaj-us-Siraj (AD 1400) writes that:

> Sultan Raziyyat—may she rest in peace!—was a great sovereign, and sagacious, just, beneficent, the patron of the learned, a dispenser of justice, the cherisher of her subjects, and of warlike talent, and was endowed with all the admirable attributes and qualifications necessary for kings; but, as she did not attain the destiny, in her creation, of being computed among men, of what advantage were all these excellent qualifications unto her? [sic][61]

In other words, he thought that though she was endowed with all the qualities befitting a king, she was not born a man, so what good did all these advantages do to her? That, of course, is for history to decide and Raziya should definitely be given her due.

However, this was not the cause of her downfall: the Turkish nobles resented her attempts to offset their power by creating a counter-nobility of the non-Turks.

She appointed Jamaluddin Yaqut, her father's slave, as *Amir e Akhur* or commander of the horses. This was taken as an affront by the Turkish nobles as, till now, it was they who held all the important posts. That the Sultan had a mind of her own was not taken too kindly by them. She also fought and defeated the rebels against her government.

The stories of romance between Raziya and Yaqut are what dominate today's telling of Raziya's life. Minhaj-us-Siraj writes that 'Yakut, the Habashi [Abyssinian or Ethiopian], who was Lord of the Stables, acquired favour in attendance upon the Sultan, so that the Turk Amirs and Maliks began to be envious there at.'[62] It was around this time that Raziya also donned male clothes and assumed the headdress of a man instead of a veil. The main 'speculative' accusations come from Abdul Malik Isami. Isami writes in *Futuhu's Salatin* (1350) that, 'I am told that a slave of Ethiopian race used to stand by her side when she mounted her horse. With one hand he used to hold her arm and help her to mount her horse firmly.'[63] That is exactly what he would have done for her father Iltutmish.

Isami, who is writing at least a century later, speculates on how the grandees of the state would have decided to seize the royal seal from her, because 'this demon (Jamaluddin Yaqut) had become more powerful in the state than other servants and could find a way to seize the royal seal.'[64] He then goes on to describe the character of women being generally weak, given to inflamed passions and deficient in intellect, thus not to be trusted with matters of statecraft.

It is these words which were exaggerated by later historians and storytellers to create a lurid romance which is all we remember this brave monarch for.

Ibn Battuta (1308–1368) writes that she 'was accused of connections with an Abyssinian slave of hers'[65] but perhaps her trust in someone who was her trusted mentor and, possibly, father figure has been misconstrued. Independent women carving their own destinies have always been suspected.

Malik Altuniya, the governor of Tabarhind (Bhatinda), rose against her and she went to battle against him. The Turkish nobles in her army mutinied, Malik Yaqut was killed and she herself was captured.

The rebellious nobles and defeated army returned to Delhi and raised her brother Bahram Shah to the throne of Delhi in April 1240. Meanwhile Altuniya, disappointed at being deprived of any reward for his rebellion, offered marriage to Raziya, who accepted it.

Raziya and Altuniya, along with an army, attacked Bahram Shah in September–October 1240. The two armies met near Delhi, an obstinate conflict ensued in which Raziya and Altunia were defeated on 14 October 1240 and driven back. When they reached Kaithal, all their soldiers deserted them and they fell into the hands of the zamindars and were massacred the same day.[66]

Minhaj-us-Siraj writes in *Tabaqat-e-Nasiri*,

Together they [Sultan Raziya and Malik Altuniya after their marriage] marched an army towards Delhi, aiming to dethrone Bahrām Shah. But the new sultan led out a force to rout his sister and Altuniya and succeeded. The troops accompanying the couple abandoned them, and both Raziya and her husband were killed by Hindus [Indians] on 25 Rabi' I 638/14 October 1240.[67]

Now for a look at the claims that this is not Sultan Raziya's tomb as there are similar claims from Tonk in Rajasthan and Kaithal in Haryana. I quote the contemporary and medieval historians before drawing my own conclusions.

Shams Siraj Afif wrote *Tarikh-e-Firozshahi,* a *History of India* during the reign (1351–1388) of Firoz Shah Tughlaq. He describes the building of the new city of Firozabad, known today as Firoz Shah Kotla. He describes the various villages and lands that were bought by the Sultan for its construction.

> The Sultán having selected a site at the village of
> Gáwín, on the banks of the Jumna, founded the city
> of Fíroz-ábád, before he went to Lakhnautí the second
> time. Here he commenced a palace ... and the nobles
> of his court having also obtained (giriftand) houses
> there, a new town sprang up, five kos distant from
> Dehlí. Eighteen places were included in this town,
> the kasba of Indarpat, the saráí of Shaikh Malik Yár
> Parán, the saráí of Shaikh Abu Bakr Túsí, the village
> of Gáwín, the land of Khetwára, the land of Lahráwat,
> the land of Andháwalí, the land of the saráí of Malika,
> the land of the tomb of Sultán Raziya, the land of
> Bhárí, the land of Mahrola, and the land of Sultánpur.
> So many buildings were erected that from the kasba
> of Indarpat to the Kúshk-i shikár, five kos apart, all
> the land was occupied.[68]

Even today, land records are considered an authentic source
of information and Afif wrote not too long after Raziya's
death.

A most surprising and detailed account is that of Ibn
Batuta who writes,[69]

> A battle took place. Raziya's troops suffered a defeat
> and she fled. Overpowered by hunger and strained
> by fatigue she repaired to a peasant whom she found
> tilling the soil. She asked him for something to eat.
> He gave her a piece of bread which she ate and fell
> asleep; and she was dressed like a man. But, while

she was asleep the peasant's eyes fell upon a gown (qaba) studded with jewels which she was wearing under her clothes. He realized that she was a woman. So he killed her, plundered her and drove away her horse, and then buried her in his field. Then he went to the market to dispose of one of her garments. But the people of the market became suspicious of him and took him to the *shihna*, that is, hakim [magistrate]. There he was beaten into confessing her murder and pointed out where he had buried her. Her body was then disinterred, washed, shrouded and buried there. A dome was built over her grave which is now visited, and people obtain blessings from it. It lies on the bank of the great river Jumna (Jun) at a distance of one parasang (farsakh) from the city.

In the thirteenth century, the river Yamuna did indeed flow in that area, and Shah Turkman Bayabani, in whose khanqah she was buried, lived in the wilderness of that area.

Sir Syed, in his book, *Asar-us-Sanadid* also refers to Sultan Raziya being buried near Turkman Gate and that she was a devotee of the saint Turkman Shah.[70]

Tonk does not figure anywhere in any narrative of any medieval historian.

Malik Yaqut was already long dead when Raziya fled Delhi, married Malik Altuniya and came back to Delhi to fight her brother and was killed, so there is no question of both of them being buried together.

In my humble opinion, the only proof which bears scrutiny is the account by Shams Siraj Afif where he talks of the land deeds of the fifth city of Delhi—Firozabad or Firoz

Shah Kotla as it is known today—and they clearly state that the land on which Sultan Raziya's tomb stands was part of the city of Firozabad. Even today, land deeds are clear proof of ownership, whether of the dead or alive.

A piece of paper proclaiming this to be the Shahi Masjid Raziya Sultan in Bulbuli Khana was posted on the wall of the mosque. Sadly, they didn't get her title right as she used Sultan Raziya—a monarch, not Raziya Sultan, which could be wife, sister or consort.

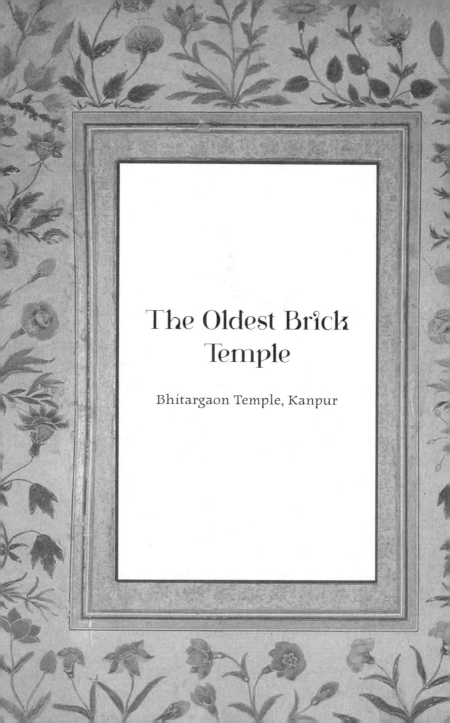

The Oldest Brick Temple

Bhitargaon Temple, Kanpur

One of the most important sources of history is architecture or built heritage. It documents the progress of man and civilizations. In India, religious and secular buildings stand as testimony to the skill and labour of its artisans and workers and the resources of the rulers and richer sections of society.

The excavations of the cities known as the Indus Valley Civilization testify to urbanization as early as 2600 BCE.

Rock-cut architecture began to develop from third century BCE and though the earliest rock-cut architecture is from the Mauryan dynasty in third century BCE, the Ajanta caves is one of the earliest rock-cut temples.

As man progressed and learnt new techniques, the rock-cut temples gave way to stone temples and as stone was not easily available everywhere, to brick temples. Brick architecture was not new, for we see their use in the Indus Valley Civilization and Buddhist monasteries. It was in the Gangetic plains with alluvial soil and paucity of stones and rocks that brick architecture flourished. Even where stone was readily available, brick was the preferred medium in North India as it had the flexibility of being made in smaller units and thus gave rise to more possibilities. But it had its restrictions, as it limited the size and made it difficult to bridge large spaces. The first group of religious brick structures was Buddhist and the second, Hindu.

The earliest of the second phase was the brick temple in Bhitargaon, near Kanpur.

Though rock-cut and stone temples withstood the vagaries of time, brick temples were not so fortunate and that is what makes the brick temple of Bhitargaon, some 50 kilometres off Kanpur in UP so special.

Bhitargaon Temple, Kanpur

Most of us who visit UP for tourism purposes, go to Lucknow, Prayagraj or Varanasi but it is in places off the beaten track such as Bhitargaon that one finds such gems. Bhitargaon literally means inner village and it is indeed in the interior of the Kanpur countryside. There is a village around it and one can ask the way to it.

I had read about this temple and was very keen to visit it and I finally got a chance in October to visit it with friends.

It is a long drive through the countryside and the temple is in the middle of a village within an ASI enclosure. It is the oldest surviving brick structure in India and extremely precious.

In 1861, Lord Canning appointed Sir Alexander Cunningham as the Archaeological Surveyor to the Government of India and it is to this remarkable man that we owe a huge debt for locating and rescuing India's built heritage. He was responsible for excavations in Sarnath in 1837 and Sanchi in 1841. In 1871, he was made the first director general of the ASI. After that began a series of field surveys which are documented in reports.

In the 'Report of the Gangetic Provinces 1875–76 and 1877–78', Cunningham writes that his friend Raja Ravi Prasada, gave him information of a brick temple near Kanpur with superior terracotta work. Between November 1877 and February 1878 he made two visits to Bhitargaon.

The village Bhitargaon had been part of an ancient city known as Phulpur. The temple was simply known as 'Dewal', or temple, by the locals. It is one of the earliest surviving brick temples of India and thus extremely important.

Though Cunningham had placed it as belonging to the seventh century, it has subsequently been identified as belonging to the late Gupta period and dated to AD fifth century.

Percy Brown calls it a 'tall tower-like edifice rising in diminishing stages', measuring it as 70 feet high, standing in the centre of a fairly high plinth.[71] The plan is 36 sq. feet in diameter double recessed angles and had a projected porch approached by steps on the east side. This porch, missing now, can be seen in a photograph by J.D. Beglar in 1878.[72] Beglar was with the ASI and was Cunningham's assistant.

Beglar's photograph shows a very dilapidated state of the temple as a lightning strike damaged it and destroyed the top of the shikhara. However, the porch can be seen very clearly. According to Cunningham's conversations with the locals, this strike happened a few years before the 'mutiny' in 1857 but no one knows the exact date.

By the time the money for its repair was sanctioned, the

outer semicircular arch over the entrance steps had also fallen down and only the one leading into the sanctum remains. The structure we see now was reconstructed from the masonry in 1905 and is different from its original shape, as it was rebuilt in unrelieved straight vertical lines. The top was left untouched as there was no evidence of its original shape.

This porch led to the interior windowless chamber which is 15 feet square.

The flooring, which must have been different earlier, is now paved with modern bricks. It has thick walls, (eight-feet wide) though not of uniform thickness on all sides, possibly due to the outer shape. There is no decoration inside except for niches to keep the images.

Today we climb steps and go directly inside as the porch has fallen down (it fell in 1895 before repairs could be done). Its small size means that it was not a temple for general worship but a shrine dedicated to a deity or a repository for an image. According to Cunningham, because of the Varaha incarnation at the back of the temple, it was probably a Vishnu temple. The central panel on the back of the temple was identified as Vishnu as Varaha (now damaged) and the next one as Vishnu and Ayudhapurusas. This panel is less damaged than the other and depicts Vishnu as eight-armed in his Trivikrama form. These two images are still present and a comparison with the 1878 images that was photographed by Beglar[73] shows that they are more or less in the same condition and there has been no further damage.

When Brown saw it, the porch was existing and he writes, 'The interior is quite plain but displays certain constructional expedients, which for a building of so early a date are of considerable interest, as the porch and cella are both covered over by domical vaults, and the passage connecting the two by a wagon-vault.[74] The porch would have been the entrance to the *ardha-mandapa*, which is present today without a roof. The ardha-mandapa is described by Cunningham as measuring eight feet by 7.3 feet.

Indeed, the entrance into the sanctum is of great interest as it shows one of the first uses of a semicircular doorway. It is however, a corbelled or false arch composed of bricks placed edge to edge instead of face to face. Cunningham calls them 'Hindu arch' as he writes it is peculiar to India.[75] This is different from a true arch, which has wedge shaped voussoirs and a triangular keystone. The corbelled arch could not support large domes whereas a true arch can.

Another important feature of this temple is its tall pyramidical spire or shikhara above the inner sanctum or *garbha-griha*. This shikhara is one of the first spires in a temple and later became the standard feature of Nagara temple architecture of India.

The walls are eight feet thick and decorated by terracotta sculptures on panels fitted into niches separated by bold ornamental pilasters made for the purpose. Many have fallen down or been damaged, many have found their way into museums.

Muhammad Zaheer, who examined this temple in the 1960s and wrote a monologue on it, titled *The Temple of Bhītargāon*, has counted 143 panels.[76]

Zaheer's work is fascinating and outstanding, for he has analysed it in great detail. Apart from the figures depicting divine figures, animals and mithunas, Zaheer has analysed the coiffeur of the 20 plaques showing only heads. When I went there, since the panels are very high up and now badly damaged, they weren't very clearly visible so I cite from his book. Out of these 18 are women; five heads are shown with short hair, parted in the middle with one coiffeur being very distinctive with 'tresses falling heavily on either side of the head,' with 'two small curls, one on either side of the forehead'.[77]

There are four heads with honeycomb coiffeurs, three with ringlets and two with streaked locks and central buns, while three have simple hairstyles which are not very prominent. And of course of the male heads, while one is bald, the other is indistinct.

Zaheer describes eight panels which show men and animals. I add these descriptions so that those who go and enjoy it, have a great experience and know that these panels describe the life of those times.

There is a panel with four men and a tiger plus some other animal. The male figure wears a short tunic and breeches with remnants of a sash being visible, writes Zaheer.

The iconographic panels include, Vishnu on Garuda (now damaged), Ganga standing on a *Makara,* accompanied by two female attendants: one attendant holds a parasol and stands on a fish, while the smaller attendant is in a crouching position. There is an extremely damaged panel which Zaheer deduces to be Goddess Yamuna because it is next to the one of Goddess Ganga and there is a parasol and bird.

The remaining ones are of Shiva and Parvati seated together, Ganesha, an eight-armed Vishnu, a Mahisasurmardini, Vishnu killing Madhu and Kaitabha (in Indian Museum, Kolkata), Sita giving alms to Ravana, Krishna wrestling, Gajalakshmi and many amphibian and animal figures as well as flora and foliage. There is a fish with an elephant head, a peacock-like bird, a man fighting an elephant, etc.

This temple and its survival is a tribute to human beings and their piety. It is worth a visit. As I walked around it, I kept marvelling at every brick and panel. In fact, the bricks used in the pilasters are also ornamented. They have chequered designs and incised lines, all placed in such a way that their designs are not interrupted. These pilasters are exquisite and plainly visible, so I walked around shooting close ups of them with my camera.

Later, when I read Zaheer's book, I learnt that each pilaster has 16 pieces consisting pedestal, shaft, capital and abacus.

There are bricks with upward-pointing lotus tips and petals.

On the way and quite close by, there's another unique stupa-like temple dedicated to lord Jagannanth in Behta Bujurg Village. The speciality of that temple, according to the priest there, is that the ceiling of the temple sanctum gets dampened seven days before monsoons arrive. It's a fail-proof barometer of monsoons according to him. In addition, he told us that if it is only moisture, there would be moderate rain, and if droplets form, there would be heavy rainfall.

Our villages and our country are a testimony to the diverse beliefs and cultures of our country as well as the skill and workmanship of our ancestors.

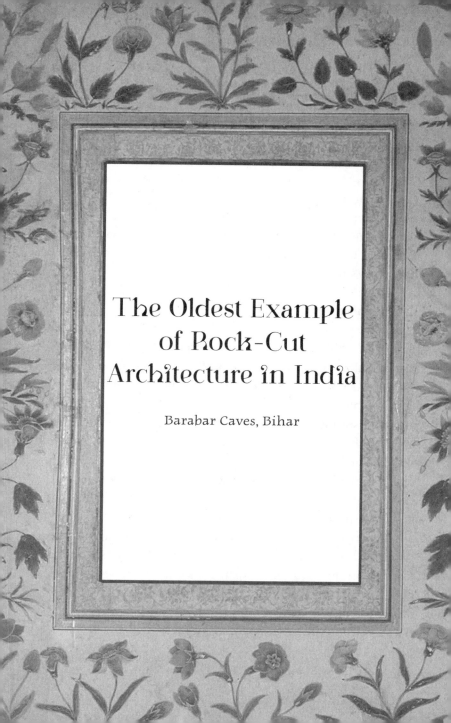

The Oldest Example of Rock-Cut Architecture in India

Barabar Caves, Bihar

One of the richest legacies of our ancient past is in the state of Bihar. It is here that Lord Buddha gained enlightenment and where the Jain Tirthankar, Lord Mahavir preached and died. Both were contemporaries and their followers built many monuments in their honour.

Bihar was also the centre of the Mauryan Empire. The entire area of Rajgir (the capital of Magadha), Bodh Gaya (where Lord Buddha gained enlightenment), Nalanda with its monastery, Pawapuri (where Lord Mahavir gained nirvana) and Gaya with its ancient past are a heritage lover's paradise. I spent a few blissful days visiting each and every historical site and soaking in the past.

But it was once more an obscure place which enthralled me the most.

A few years ago, I attended a lecture by Prof. Irfan Habib on Indian architecture. He started with the Barabar Hill Caves, in particular the one called Lomas Rishi, which are the oldest surviving rock-cut caves in India. I had been wanting to visit it since that day. I hired a car and talked to a guide in the area and set off. I was the only visitor there, and had it not been for the locals, I could possibly have been the only person there. Which is why, it is best for any solo traveller, especially women, to hire a local guide. These caves are also kept locked so one has to go through the ASI office located at the foot of the Barabar Hill to ensure that the guard opens it.

The word Barabar is said to be a derivation of Bara Awar or great enclosure, but according to Kuraishi,[78] 'the inscription on the Lomas Rishi cave calls it the Piavaragiri-guha, and though Pravara literally means great, it might perhaps be taken as the proper name of the hill. From Pravara, Barabar would be an easy corruption.'[79]

Barabar Caves: Lomas Rishi entrance

The Barabar group of granite hills have several distinct peaks with a valley and water body. To the south of them, there exists a low range of granite hills, some 500 feet long, 100 feet wide and 30 feet high that runs from east to west. It is in these twin hills of Barabar and Nagarjuni in the Makhdumpur region of the Jehanabad district of Bihar that these caves are situated: Barabar (four caves) and Nagarjuni (three caves). While three of the Barabar caves were excavated under Ashoka, the Nagarjuni were excavated under his grandson Dashratha.

The crocodile-shaped hill which houses three caves: the Karna Chaupar cave, the Sudama cave and the Lomas Rishi cave next to it are the oldest surviving rock-cut caves in India, dating back to Emperor Ashoka. He built it for the Ajivika sect. The Sudama cave is nearby. It must be kept in mind that these names are not the original names but have come up much later, perhaps in the medieval age. These were excavated under the Mauryan rulers and were meant for the Ajivika sect or Buddhist monks. They were used as Brahmanical shrines in AD fourth century when King Sardula Varma placed images of Deva Mata, Katyayani and Mahadeva in three of them.[80]

The highest hill here in the Barabar range is the Siddhesvar Hill and has a Baba Siddhnath Temple, also known as the Shiva Temple/Siddheshwar Nath Temple. The temple was built during the Gupta period in seventh century CE. The local legends attribute the construction of the temple to Bana Raja (the father-in-law of the legendary king Jarasandha of Rajgir).

The Ajivikas were a sect of ascetics, said to have been established in fifth century BCE by Makkhali Gosala. They believed in the doctrine of absolute determinism, that is, there is no such thing as free will and everything is predetermined by pre-existing causes in the cosmos.

The walk up the hills to the caves is also very interesting as it is through beautiful scenery of lush green trees and vegetation on the granite hills.

KARAN CHAUPAR CAVE

The first cave that one comes to is called Karan Chaupar or Supiya-Graha, which is how it is referred to in the inscription on its walls.

It is kept locked to prevent damage and the guide called the guard to open it. There were many coins thrown at the entrance as locals believe in the wishing power of the cave. There is a mound opposite the entrance with some later

Buddhist sculptures and a Shivalinga.

The Sidheshvar Hill is opposite this and the Shiva temple can be accessed from the steps in front of it.

The Karna Chaupar Cave is a simple rectangular hall measuring 33 feet six inches by 14 feet. The walls are six feet one inch in height and have a vaulted roof rising four feet eight inches above the walls. At the right, or the west end, is a low platform as if for the placement of an image, and the walls are polished smooth. This cave has no architectural feature of importance and its primary importance lies in the inscriptions on the right of the entrance. This records the excavation of the cave in the nineteenth year after the coronation of Ashoka (244–45 BC).

> Asoka is the earliest author who has left us texts written on stone in any comprehensible Indian script. There may have been reports about similar inscriptions in Achaemenid Iran; in India, however, Asoka had no local precursor in this respect and, therefore, he had to experience many difficulties in the beginning.[81]

The inscription suffered damage over the centuries and Harry Falk has deciphered it as:

> When king Priyadarsin had been anointed nineteen years, he went to Jalutha and then this cave (called) Supriyeksa was given to the Ajivikas.[82]

There are also several short inscriptions on the jambs of the doorway from the Gupta period which refer to Bodhimula 'the root of Intelligence', and Daridra Kundra 'the cave of the poor' or 'the mendicant's cave.'

For those interested in literature, this area was also the setting for the opening of E.M. Forster's *A Passage to India*.

THE SUDAMA CAVE

A short walk up to the crocodile and we come to the Sudama cave. I am anxious and restless to see the carved arch of the Lomas Rishi cave but my guide asks me to have patience.

The entrance is on the opposite side of the Karna Chaupar Cave.

The doorway, which was left incomplete for some reason, is sunk in a recess six sq. feet and two feet deep. On the eastern wall of this recess of porch, there is an inscription of two lines with Pali characters. The polished granite finish of the cave starts from here. An attempt had been made to obliterate the greater part of this inscription with a chisel but owing to the great depth of the letters, the work of destruction was not an easy one, and the clearly cut lines of the original letters, with the exception of one, perhaps at the end, are still distinctly traceable in the midst of the rough holes made by the destroyer's chisel.[83]

By King Priyadarsin, in the 12th year of his reign, this cave of Banyans was offered to the Ajivikas.[84]

The excavation of this cave, therefore, dates as far back as 252 BCE and consists of two chambers. The first is a long rectangular room in which one enters and is 32 feet nine inches in length, by 19 feet six inches in breadth and the walls are six feet nine inches high with the vaulted roof adding another five feet six inches to it, making it 12 feet three inches.

The inner chamber accessed through a door cut in the

rock is nearly circular with a hemispherical domed roof. Perhaps this was a meditation cave. This roof also projects into the outer chamber and is cut in a style as if to represent a thatched roof. The inner room is 19 feet 11 inches in diameter from west to east and 19 feet from north to south. There was a shallow recess on the eastern side as if to make a statue or niche but it was left incomplete. The walls here are also rough compared to the highly polished granite finish of the outer room. Work was abandoned, perhaps, as they reached a deep fissure which forms one of the natural lines of the cleavage of the rock.

As I stood there, my guide asked me to close my eyes and feel the reverberation in that room as he recited some Buddhist prayers. I can't describe my feelings. I can only say that I was transported to a different world.

On the western wall of the outer room there were drawings of horses.

The caves are so well polished that you can see your reflection on the cave (and its dark inside).

My granite kitchen slabs don't shine as much as these 2,500-year-old cave surfaces do.

Of course vandalism has meant that some people have tried to scratch it to see what's underneath.

LOMAS RISHI CAVE

Finally, I stood in front of the arched entrance which decorates the cover of many a book on Indian architecture.

The Lomas Rishi Cave is the oldest known example of rock-cut caves and architecture. Its entrance is special.

On the entrance doorway, a beautifully carved row of

elephants proceed towards votive stupa emblems along the curved architrave or door frame, very similar to the structural chaityas of that period.

This is the earliest survival of the ogee or horseshoe shaped arch also known as *gavaksha chandrashala* arch that were copied from wooden doorways and are an important part of Indian rock-cut architecture.

There are no Ashoka period inscriptions here. There is, however, an inscription above the entrance doorway from fifth century CE by the Maukhari dynasty ruler, King Anantavarman. It is called Pravaragiriguha or 'The Great Mountain Cave' in the inscription.

While the interior of the cave is very similar to the Sudama Cave, the roof and floor inside has been left unfinished and rough. The outer hall is 33 feet by 19 feet. The cave leads to a circular meditation cave where one can see the markings of the carvers on the rock.

The fourth cave here is called Vishwamitra or Vishwa Jhopri cave and has an Ashokan inscription which places it in the twelfth year of his reign and offered to the Ajivikas. It is away from the main hill and is a simple rectangular room with an elongated porch and a semicircular room inside the main room and can be accessed through a narrow trapezoidal passage.

The Nagarjuni Caves are a short drive or a 10-minute walk away. They are high up in the hill with steps hewn in the hill face leading up to them. These were excavated during the reign of Dashratha Maurya (232–224 BC), grandson of Ashoka.

I found climbing the steps quite adventurous and apart from visiting the cave, it also gives a vantage view of the countryside. I visited only one cave here on the southern side, named Gopika Cave. It is the largest and the first cave that one accesses after climbing up. It is 45 feet five inches long and 19 feet two inches wide, with semicircular ends.

The inscription records it as the Gopika's Cave, an abode lasting as the Sun and Moon, caused to be excavated by Dashratha, beloved of the Devas, on his accession to the throne as a hermitage for the most devoted Ajivikas.

There is a long inscription called the Gopika Cave inscription that was added by King Anantavarman in fifth century CE.

The two other caves are on the north side and are called Vahiyaka and Vedathika and are very small.

These are not only aesthetically important but historically of great importance too as they provided a prototype for the larger Buddhist Chaitya halls found in Maharashtra and influenced South Asian rock-cut architecture.

They are a tribute to man's endeavour, dedication and skill and, therefore, not to be missed.

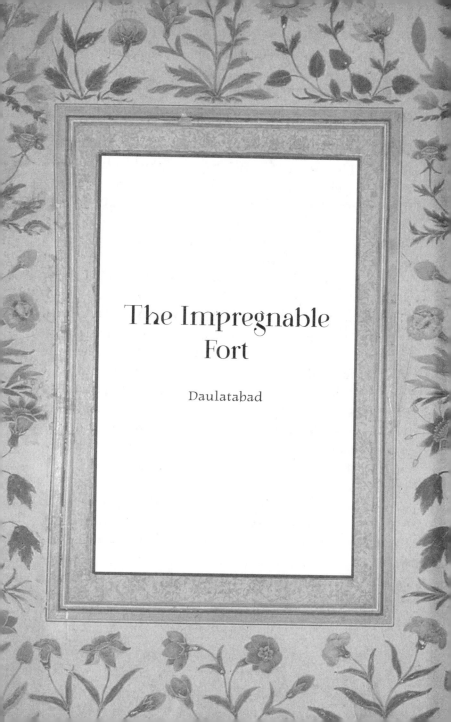

The Impregnable Fort

Daulatabad

The Moroccan traveller Ibn Batuta, who visited Daulatabad in 1340 with Sultan Muhammad bin Tughlaq, praising the impregnability of the Daulatabad Fort, writes, 'The fortress of Deogir of which we have spoken is a rock standing alone in a plain. It was cut smooth and on its summit was built the stronghold which is reached by means of a leather ladder which is taken away during the night.'[85] Indeed, it seems to rise perpendicularly from a cone-shaped hill and looks a daunting climb for any visitor.

Today, because of the habitation and construction all around it, it is difficult to imagine its isolated grandeur, but a pencil drawing of the town and fort of Dejouri (Deogiri or Daulatabad) by Alexander Nash (1834–1846)[86] and William Daniell[87] between 1844 and 1845 showcases it. The Daniell painting, like all the others in his series of Oriental Scenery painted during the eighteenth century, tell of a built heritage that has suffered immeasurable damage over the years.

I had read the history of the fort and the various anecdotes attached to it and was determined to explore it. Very few visitors climb up all the way to the top, so I engaged a guide and set about the task, thinking of the people who built it, the rulers who inhabited it and the invaders who sought to capture it.

It has a long history and several rulers and dynasties have added to the fortifications and buildings of the fort. The fortified citadel of Deogir/Devgiri was the capital of the Yadava dynasty who ruled the area from the ninth to the fourteenth century. The dynasty was established by Bhillama V between 1185 and 1187, after he declared independence from the Western Chalukya kingdom.

The Yadava, Hoysala and Kakatiya kingdoms, which grew in importance after the fall of the Chalukyan Empire, fought many wars amongst themselves. Deogir grew in power and was famous for its wealth. In 1292, when Alauddin Khilji attacked Deogir, catching the Yadava king Ramachandra unawares, King Ramachandra took refuge in the fort. He had to ultimately surrender when provisions ran out and had to pay a huge ransom. Deogir, with its famed riches, was always vulnerable to the demands of the Delhi sultans, and Alauddin Khilji's successor Qutbuddin Mubarak Shah finally annexed it in 1317 ending the Yadava dynasty. He named it Qutbabad.

The famed transfer of the capital of Sultan Muhammad bin Tughlaq from Delhi to Daulatabad (city of fortune), as Deogir was renamed under him, has been described by all contemporary historians. Muhammad bin Tughlaq saw Daulatabad as a strategic point from where he could rule his kingdom, which now included the Deccan. He ordered the nobles, the elite, the clergy, the mystics, the craftsmen and artisans to shift to Daulatabad. It was a 40-day journey and many perished on the way, despite the road being lined with willow trees and rest houses being provided along the way.

It was here that the sultan gave the orders for introduction of a token currency. Both these grandiose schemes came to no good and the capital established at Daulatabad was abandoned in 1334 when the people were asked to return to Delhi.

Many stayed back, notably the mystics, and Khuldabad nearby is known as the Valley of Saints with about 1,300 saints buried there.

Daulatabad was then annexed by the Bahmani

kingdom (1347–1527) and after the breakup of the Bahmani kingdom by its offshoot, the Nizamshahis of Ahmadnagar captured it in 1499.

The fortress of Daulatabad was besieged by the Mughal emperor Shah Jahan and it became a part of the Mughal Empire in 1633. A glorious painting of the siege in the *Padshahnama* depicts the fort. The text describes its impregnability and fortifications as being renowned throughout the world and goes on to describe the difficulties presented by the fortress:

> This mighty fortification is in reality nine fortresses situated [on] a splendid granite mountain of the utmost magnitude and height in the midst of a flat plain. Four of the fortresses are on top of the mountain, one above the other, and all around the mountain is a wide, deep, water-filled moat carved from the granite. The other five mighty fortresses and two deep moats adjoin the mountain.[88]

Aurangzeb spent much of his years in the Deccan, either in Aurangabad or the fort of Daulatabad.

After the death of Aurangzeb, many provincial governors established their own power centres. Aurangabad, along with Daulatabad Fort, came in the territory of Nizam-ul-Mulk of Hyderabad who had established what was virtually an independent kingdom. In 1760, the fort, along with some other portions of the Nizam's holdings, came under the Marathas but in 1780, the Nizam took control of it once again.

The fort is an amazing place where an interested visitor can unravel centuries of mysteries and history. As I walked up, I tried to imagine the famed impregnability of the fort.

Its walls built initially by the Yadavas were added to by the Khiljis, Tughlaqs amd Bahmanis and the Nizamshahi rulers.

Dr Dulari Qureishi, writes that, 'the fort according to the Indian ancient texts falls under the classification of *Misra durg* or mixed fort as it combines the qualities of a *Giridurg* (mountain fort) and a *Deva Durga* (God's Fort) and *Bhumi durg* (land fort).'[89]

There are a number of tenth -and eleventh-century Jain and Hindu cave temples in the hill and it was a popular religious site. I visited one on my way up to the top most flag staff tower.

The outer wall, which enclosed the citadel, is 4.43 kilometres in circumference and between it and the base of the citadel there are three lines of fortifications. There are several walls in between the outer citadel wall and the fort itself, entered through a series of lofty gateways. These walls had their own bastions, battlements, moats and devices to repel the enemy by those guarding it. The moats would have drawbridges for easy negotiation by the soldiers and inmates of the fort and drawn up in times of attack. Today there is an iron causeway over it.

The most remarkable features of the fort are the moat and the scarp all hewn out of solid rock. The moat is about 100 feet deep and though now it looks harmless with a little rainwater in it, at one time it was always kept filled with water to discourage the enemy. The Bahmanis played a major role in fortifying the fort and the moat was added by them at the base of the hill. They also built more ramparts and made the scarp sharper and more perpendicular.

The outermost of these inner walls is Ambar Kot, named after Malik Ambar, the famous Abyssinian commander of the

Nizamshahi dynasty, and its construction is attributed to him.

The wall has 45 bastions and nine principal gateways. The gateways are Fatehabad Darwaza, Nizam Shahi Darwaza, Paithan Darwaza, Kirti Darwaza, Naroti Darwaza, Kabdi Darwaza, Katgar Darwaza, Delhi or Rauza Darwaza and Khas Darwaza, all flanked by semicircular or octagonal bastions.[90]

The other lines of defence are the Mahakot or outer wall of the fort and then the parkota or barbicans.

The second fortified wall has 21 bastions to the northeast and nine bastions to the northwest, with the wall measuring 4,000 feet.[91]

And if these were not enough, there were ranges of bronze cannons to defend the fort. A bastion now houses the famous Daulatabad Mendha cannon, so called because of the ram's head crowning it. Its original name was Qila Shikan or Destroyer of Forts. It was forged for Aurangzeb and his name is inscribed on it by Muhammad Hussain Arab. The cannon is 21.6 feet (6.6 metres) in length and elaborately decorated with vegetal and geometric designs.

As I negotiated my way with the help of my guide, I was literally overwhelmed by the grandeur of it all. The massive wooden gates were provided with spikes to prevent the use of elephants for ramming into them to break them down. Some of them are still intact.

Indeed, when one looks at the hill from afar we can see that the hillside has been scarped all around to make it impossible to scale. This scarping has been done till a height of 150 feet.

For me, the climb was tiring but not difficult. Mahdi Hasan quoting the Archaeological Department, Hyderabad, in his notes in the translation of the Rehla writes,

Behind the scarp the ascent to the citadel consists of a spiral passage cut in the heart of the rock in a most ingenious fashion, containing numerous secret chambers for the accommodation of guards. The upper outlet of the passage is fitted with an iron grating on which when necessary a large fire could be kindled to smother the enemy.

As one comes out of the gateways, the first thing you see in all its glory is the Chand Minar. The guide, of course, waxed eloquently about its comparison to the Qutub Minar in Delhi; though there is no comparison with the grandeur of the Qutub, this is in no way less. It was built as a victory tower by Sultan Alauddin Bahman Shah in 1425 to mark his conquest of Daulatabad. It rises up to a height of 210 feet and has four storeys, which are surrounded by balconies. Remnants of blue tiles can be seen. There is a small mosque attached to it.

Along the way I passed by the hathi *hauz* and went into the Bharat Mata Mandir. This was a huge Jain Mandir, then converted into a Jama Masjid under Qutbuddin Khilji and is now a temple dedicated to Bharat Mata. After Independence, an idol of Bharat Mata was installed and the temple was dedicated to her. It has a domed entrance on the west and two arched openings in the north and south.

On the way up, picturesque in its desolation, we passed by Chini Mahal. Lying in ruins today, this used to be a beautiful palace with yellow and blue glazed tiles on its facade built by the Nizam Shahi rulers. It is now in ruins, but one can imagine its beauty and the pain of its royal prisoner, Sultan Abul Hasan Tana Shah who was imprisoned here in

1687, after Aurangzeb conquered his kingdom of Golconda. It has two floors and is falling apart and is in need of urgent repairs.

Abdul Tana Shah, also a mystic poet, was buried in the dargah of Hazrat Raju Qattal in nearby Khuldabad after his death in 1699.

When one is visiting monuments, one has to keep in mind that not all the portions are open for visitors. I could not visit Sonehri Mahal or Rang Mahal which was undergoing conservation work and could only peep through the cracks.

But what I did see, and that was thanks to the guide, was a dark passage that had to be negotiated to reach the fort. To reach this we walked over the moat and we were lucky that we had a bridge and friendly ASI guards, and not soldiers ready to defend their master's empire by shooting arrows or cannons at us.

After the bridge is a gallery built by Aurangzeb and to reach it one has to pass through a dark passage. This passage was cut out of the rock as a tunnel, with guard rooms around it. It looks innocuous enough from the outside with a teak door but once inside it's not for the faint-hearted, especially when your guide is describing how the enemy was lured inside this passage and hot oil was poured on them! There is also the dank stale air and smell of bats which makes one gag. However, always being up to a challenge, I went into every nook and cranny of this passage, climbing up and down the steps and passageways. If the enemy was still undeterred, my guide informed me, that the soldiers blew in smoke from inlets provided to choke them.

They could also be thrown into the moat where crocodiles were waiting to welcome them by opening hidden trapdoors.

Never was I as happy to come out into the open air and sunlight as that day!

The smoke as tactic used against the enemy is well documented and Qureishi writes that this was an ingenuous and effective defence technique used in this tunnel. She quotes Raunaq Ali,

> The shutter is ½ in thickness, which was used for barring the ingress of the besiegers. The plate was laid across the opening and a huge fire kindled upon it, so that it became red hot and rendered all approach to it from the inner gallery impossible. At a point about halfway through where the tunnel passed, here the vertical face of the rock hole measuring 5 feet in diameter was cut through for the fire in an iron brazier which was installed in a small chamber opening into the tunnel. When the fire was kindled the current of air from the hole would waft the smoke up the tunnel and render its passage impossible.[92]

The view from there is spectacular and I feasted on it in readiness for the rest of the stiff climb up.

We stopped at the Ganesh temple on the side and were given sugar candy and water by the lady looking after it to revive ourselves. After that we reached the Baradari built by Shah Jahan.

The Baradari, a favourite selfie point, is still very attractive with its white arches visible from far as it's on the summit of the hill and acts as an incentive to make the climb. It was built in 1636 as the imperial residence by Shah Jahan.

It is approached through a courtyard with galleries and

arcades running around it. The Baradari is octagonal in shape and built of black stone. The arched openings, with a breathtaking view of the fortress, are plastered white and stand out.

The Mughals also built a huge palace complex built at the base of the hill in the northwest corner of the Mahakot grounds. These are now in ruins and I found them inaccessible. These contained assembly halls, hammams and gardens.

The complex is huge and needs more than a day to see it all. I tried to see as much as I could. My visit culminated at the flagstaff tower where another bronze cannon is ensconced. The tower is circular and has a narrow staircase leading up to it. Thanks to my excitement to reach the highest point of the fort, I climbed up without any problems. It was only when coming down that my vertigo kicked in. I still remember the painful descent, which I made by sitting down on the steps and coming down it in that position as I couldn't stand without getting giddy from the height.

But it was worth it!

Everyone who gazes on it comes to the conclusion that this cannot be the work of man. For neither is the physical strength of mere mortals adequate to the task of such stupendous excavating and quarrying; nor in the present age, is their span of life sufficiently long to admit of their completing so vast an undertaking.

—The *Shah Jahan Nama*[93]

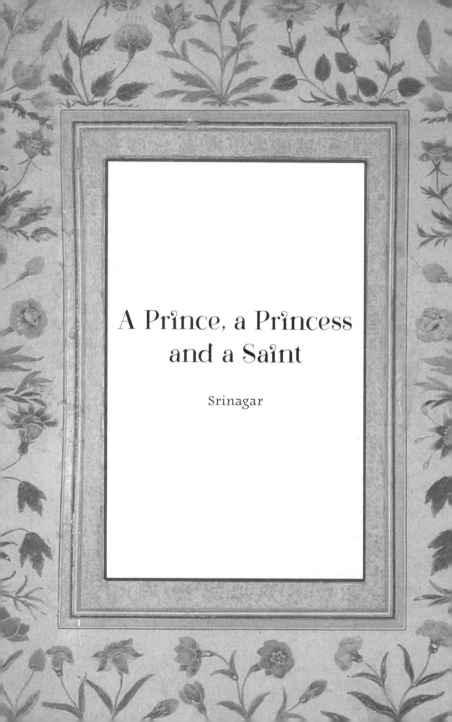

A Prince, a Princess
and a Saint

Srinagar

Kashmir with its woods, vales, hills and mountains, traditionally adopted wooden architecture. This was a common practice in the hill districts of India as well as Nepal, thanks to a limitless supply of timber. These wooden masterpieces (mostly with wood from the Deodar tree) were fantastic in shape and far more picturesque with exquisite carvings as opposed to buildings in more permanent and more intractable materials.

Even today, most hill houses are built using timber. Unfortunately, the impermanence of the material means that not much survives. One of the most beautiful examples of it is Shah Hamadan's mosque built on the banks of river Jhelum during the reign of Sultan Sikander (1389–1413). Here, of course, apart from the delicacy of the wood architecture, we have the paper mache technique brought by the Sufi Saint to the valley, embellishing the wooden surface. Another is the Jami Masjid, again built during Sultan Sikander's reign but imperilled a number of times because of fire. What we see today was built at the end of the seventeenth century.

Stone masonry was hardly used during the reign of the Kashmir Sultanate (1339–1587). We have remains of stone temples, as in the Sun Temple of Martand, but many of these were destroyed—some by nature and many by the new rulers, who did not approve of idol worship. The Martand Sun Temple, near Anantnag, of which only ruins survive, is very famous and needs no introduction. Even in this state, one can witness its majesty and grandeur as it stands well on an elevated plateau, with an immensely picturesque view of a great part of the valley.

In 1588, Kashmir was conquered by the Mughals and that began a new phase of construction. The Mughals, with their predilection for gardens, built the beautiful gardens of Shalimar and Nishat Bagh in Srinagar and many others in other parts of Kashmir.

Our journey begins with a young prince who was in search of a Sufi master to help him on his mystical journey into the world of *tassawuf*.

The Mughal emperors were always respectful and connected to Sufi saints but it culminated in Prince Dara Shukoh's (1615–1659) journey on the mystical path and his masterful treatises.

He finally found a master in Miyan Mir (1550–1635), the Qadriya saint, someone who had impressed his grandfather, Emperor Jahangir. The young prince Dara Shukoh came in touch with Miyan Mir, the celebrated Sufi saint in 1634 when he went with his father Emperor Shah Jahan to Lahore. The emperor went to meet the saint and took Dara with him. The prince had been ailing and the emperor beseeched the saint to look after him.

> Miyan Mir grasped the prince's hand and, with the other hand, picked up a clay pot that he regularly used for drinking. After filling it with water, he breathed a prayer over it and recited the fatiha. He then instructed Dar Shukoh to drink the water and said he would be cured within a week.[94]

The Prince visited Miyan Mir again while returning from Kashmir and thus began a 'harmonious communion of elevated souls'.[95] Dara became his 'de facto' disciple for the short period in which the saint was alive.

Miyan Mir passed away in 1635 and the young prince

then sought out his disciple Mullah Shah Badakshi to be his spiritual preceptor. Mulla Shah had left his homeland Badakshan[96] on a spiritual quest and became Miyan Mir's disciple.

When the young prince continued his journey to Kashmir from Lahore, he was eager to meet Shah Muhammad, popularly known as Mullah Shah Badakshi or Akhund Shah. Dara went to meet the prince and paid his obeisance and though he wanted to serve the saint as his disciple, he did not initiate the process then.

Mullah Shah was known for his secular approach and that must have influenced Dara. Though earlier Mullah Shah only spent summers in Kashmir, after Mian Mir's passing, he settled permanently in Srinagar, residing in a small cell in the mountain famous as Hari Parbat or Koh-i-Maran. His meditation was done in darkness.

In 1640, Dara Shukoh completed his biography of Sufi saints, named *Safinat-ul-Auliya* (*The Ship of Saints*) and the same year they set of again for Kashmir as part of their father's imperial entourage. On this trip, Dara Shukoh visited Mullah Shah again one night. Though the saint rebuffed him initially as he didn't want to have anything to do with emperors and princes, seeing Dara's sincere devotion towards him, he relented.

Prof. Fatima Zehra Bilgrami writes in her book *History of the Qadiri Order in India* that when Mullah Shah saw the prince he asked for a lamp to be lit and recited the following verse:

*In this desolate cell of ours we do not have a candle
As the fire of your Love illuminates our abode.*

Akhund Shah Mosque, Srinagar

Dara Shukoh requested Mullah Shah that 'they want to come to his *halqa*, and they helped him in all possible ways and built a khanqah and a house for him,' writes Bilgrami.[97]

Later, his sister Princess Jahanara Begum, following him, also became his disciple. However, in view of her purdah and propriety, she exchanged only notes with him and though on her request she once did see him as he sat under a tree and she passed by on her elephant, there was no physical contact between the two.

After Dara Shukoh and Jahanara returned from Kashmir they kept up their correspondence with the saint and stayed connected with him.

Along with his intellectual pursuits and fulfilment of royal duties, Dara Shukoh also extended his patronage to architecture. He shared his father's passion for it.[98] He sent one of his aides, Tawakkul Beg, to oversee his building projects in Kashmir.

Tawakkul Beg also wrote a book chronicling the life and times of Mullah Shah and he describes the building of the Pari Palace.[99]

Here I quote Gandhi, who describes in her book that,

'Beg describes a mountain named Koh-i Pak (Pure Mountain) overlooking the Dal Lake. From it flowed two springs, namely Salma and Qatalna.' The Chashm-e Shahi (The Shah's Spring), named after the saint, built by Jahanara Begum below is built around the Salma spring.

Unlike the traditional wood architecture of Kashmir, the royal siblings used rubble masonry. The prince constructed a beautiful six-level terrace building dedicated to Mullah Shah. The terraces were aligned in the north-south direction.

In contrast to the famous Mughal Gardens in Srinagar, this garden did not have running water streams and cascades of bubbling water and spouting chutes. Instead, the tanks in it were fed by underground water pipes, perhaps to signify inner resourcefulness and outward calm, so necessary for a man with spiritual inclinations. The Salma Spring also bubbled out in a marble tank. This would probably be the water tank that I found on the sixth and uppermost level. The tank is set in the mountain slope and would have received water from the spring above. Today it is dry.

It commands an outstanding view of Srinagar and an ideal time to be there is when the sun is setting on the Dal lake.

It is brightly lit and visible from the city, twinkling like a fairy palace.

Fittingly, the approach road to it is from the Chasm-e-Shahi and opens on to the level of the fourth terrace. A domed double archway leads one inside and then one has to make the choice of going up or down! I decided to climb up the steps provided at each level, and then make my way down the six levels, very much like a spring would do, of course minus the spring in my step, for though water may flow with ease, a mere mortal has to make an effort to climb up and down.

There is a baradari which is built in a way to cover the fifth and sixth level. The rubble masonry walls on each level are set with arched recesses.

The fifth level also has a water tank. These must have been provided with fountains which are now missing. Many visitors I saw went away from the fourth level itself as they could peep down the other three. These levels are quite simple and it must have been the upper levels that served as living space for the saint or the royal guests.

For me, there was a sense of peace but it wasn't shared by Walter Rooper Lawrence, who visited Kashmir in 1889 and wrote a book in 1985 named *The Valley of Kashmir*.

He says,

> Strange tales are told of the Pari Mahal, of the wicked magician who spirited away kings' daughters in their sleep, how an Indian princess by the order of her father brought away a *chenar* leaf to indicate the abode of her seducer, and how all the outraged kings of India seized the magician.[100]

In between their visits to Kashmir, the royal siblings invited their spiritual master to Lahore and he was pleased with the respect, care and courtesies extended to him.

He was now 'comfortable enough with the imperial family to make his own needs known.'[101] He thus desired for a khanqah, or Sufi hospice, for his disciples to stay and a congregational mosque attached to it where he could conduct the Friday prayers. He was already residing in a house on the Koh-i-Maran and a mosque and khanqah near it would be convenient for him.

He thus 'instructed Jahanara Begum's deputy in Kashmir to gather stones for construction'. The official repurposed a heap of stones originally belonging to an idol temple (*butkhana*). 'Tell your mistress to make a khanqah for God.' A sum of ₹60,000 was released for the construction of the masjid-khanqah.[102]

It took a couple of years to build and in 1651, when Shah Jahan visited Kashmir, it is said that he visited the saint. Meanwhile, Mulla Shah again visited Lahore and gifted his imperial hosts with a manuscript of his poems.

Gandhi writes that:

Jahanara's attendants gave the shaikh a valuable diamond which he apparently accepted. The mosque-khanqah complex was commemorated by Mulla Shah with a verse and chronogram:

Of stone did Begum Sahib make a building
The noble child of the faith-protecting emperor of the
worlds

Ending with the chronogram:
The date of my khanqah is khanqah-i Shah[103]

This mosque was in ruins when I went and seemed to be rarely visited. I had read about it as Akhund Shah's masjid on a scarp in Hari Parbat in 1649 and also that Dara Shukoh had built it. Since it is very close to Makhdoom Saheb's dargah on a higher spot on Hari Parbat, I could see the remnants of a few petals of the lotus finial, which is supposed to be the only one on a mosque in Kashmir.

Fortunately, I could see that repairs were underway by the ASI.

It's in a large rectangular enclosure with a tank for ablutions, surrounded by apartments for devotees and servants.

The mosque itself is a simple and elegant building of grey granite slabs over brickwork, much of which is now exposed. There were some children playing under a large, leafy chinar tree and an old man sitting there. After much persuasion and telling him that I was researching monuments, I was allowed by the ASI guard to enter inside.

On the entrance of the mosque, below the chronogram mentioned above, I found these lines in Arabic.

wa man dakhalahoo kaana aaminaa

whoever enters it shall be safe

(These lines are from the Quran 3:97 and refer to the Ka'ba in Mecca)

The second line reads:

wallahu mufattihul abwaab

Allah is the opener of doors

The facade with the tree is beautiful and once inside, I saw that it was built around a huge courtyard with rooms on all four sides. This was probably for the madrasa students. A lofty central *pishtaq* in the west-facing aisle led me to the mihrab. The scalloped arches of the doorway in the pishtaq are trademark Shah Jahan architectural style and a stark reminder of the impermanence of life.

While Mullah Shah remained safe from the wrath of Aurangzeb and died a natural death in 1661 in Lahore, Dara Shukoh was executed by Aurangzeb in 1659, after the latter won the war of succession.

The mosque remains a mute testimony to

a unique coming together of three individuals in establishing a new language of mosque architecture in Kashmir. Inspired by local geography, the mosques that Dārā, Mullā Shāh and Jahān Ārā patronized were uniquely situated within a setting of terraced gardens, for which Kashmir was famed at the imperial court. Under the influence of their spiritual masters, Mullā Shāh, the royal siblings helped in expanding the scope of this terrestrial paradise from a royal retreat of sensual pleasure into a setting for spiritual retreat. The change in the political climate at the imperial court, with Dārā's execution, resulted in abandonment of this architectural experiment as well as the mosque of Mullā Shāh. Soon after, the saint would be recalled to Lahore and the numerous buildings associated with him in Kashmir would stand abandoned, forgotten and forlorn.[104]

As always, ruins make for wonderful photography and I took my fill, while the heritage lover in me cried at its ruinous condition.

.Today, one can only make out that this mosque must have been quite a huge complex from the ruins of the cells for devotees and visitors, the remnants of the madrasa, the hammam and the stones.

As I walked around the complex, outside I could see a gurudwara and a dove flying in the distance.

I hope the prince and princess are at peace too.

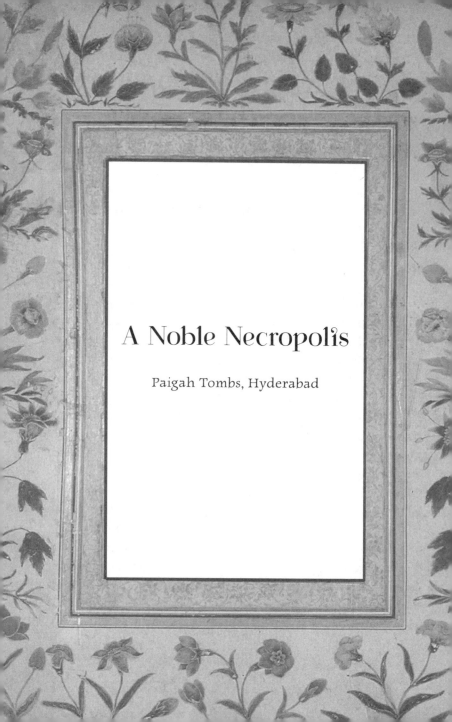

A Noble Necropolis

Paigah Tombs, Hyderabad

Today, the city of Hyderabad is the capital of Andhra Pradesh and Telangana. The Deccan, as the entire area where this city is located was called, has an ancient past with excavated finds from the Iron Age. Some of the dynasties that ruled the region were the Kakatiyas, the Bahmanis, the Qutb Shahi, the Mughals and finally the Asaf Jahi dynasty in 1724 by Asaf Jah I before being taken over by the Mughal governor of the Deccan, Nizam-ul Mulk, who later became independent. It was finally merged with the Union of India after Independence.

The Qutb Shahi kingdom was a famous Deccan kingdom, founded by the Qutb Shahi rulers, after the disintegration of the Bahmani Kingdom.

Hyderabad is a 500-year-old city with a historical and modern past. It was founded by Sultan Muhammad Quli Qutb Shah, the fifth Qutb Shahi ruler in 1591. Incidentally, Muhammad Quli Qutb Shah (1580–1611 CE) is considered one of the first poets of the Urdu language and was the first to have a published *diwan* in Urdu.

The original city, now known as Old Hyderabad, was on the banks of the river Musi but like many other historic cities built on rivers, the river has shifted course. If Old Hyderabad is home to the magnificent Charminar, Mecca Masjid, Hussain Sagar Lake, Falaknuma Palace and the Qutb Shahi tombs, modern Hyderabad is home to multinational IT firms and has earned the nickname of Cyberabad.

There are two versions of the name Hyderabad:

According to popular legend, Muhammad Quli Qutb Shah fell in love with a dancing girl named Bhagyavati or Bhagmati and built a city in her honour, naming it Bhagyanagaram. However, when the girl accepted Islam she was given the

Paigah Tombs

Paigah Tombs

A Saint, a Folk Tale and Other Stories

title of Hyder Begum and the city became Hyderabad. The Charminar was also built by Muhammad Quli Qutb Shah as a ceremonial gateway into the city. The more plausible explanation is that the Qutb Shahi rulers were devout adherents of Shia Islam and named it after Ali ibn Abi Talib, whose title is Hyder. Hazrat Ali, as he is popularly known amongst the Shias, was the Prophet's son-in-law and the fourth Caliph. He is famous for his bravery and statesmanship.

The city is multicultural and we find many iconic temples, mosques and churches situated here. Its cuisine is also very famous and normally one thinks of haleem and biryani, the two signature dishes of the city, or the beautiful and lofty Charminar or the palaces of the erstwhile Nizam who was the richest man in the world at one point in time. If you are interested in clothes, then Hyderabad has the unique khada dupatta and its accompanying necklaces. One would rarely relate Hyderabad to an exquisite necropolis hidden away in the heart of the city.

The land was divided into tenures named as jagirs, which meant that the revenue of the tract of land, assigned to different nobles, went to them. This was started by the Delhi sultans and carried on till Independence.

The nobles not only collected revenue, but also administered it for the period that it was given to him for. It was a feudal land grant system. There were two types of jagirs: conditional and non-conditional. In the case of conditional jagirs, one of the conditions was that the jagirdar had to maintain troops who would serve the royal army as and when required.

The jagirs assigned to the first Nawab, Shams-ul-Omra, by Nizam Asaf Jah, in lieu of payment for maintaining the

Nizam's household troops, were known as Paigah. The Paigah jagirs comprised an area of about 3,827 square kilometres, which included 1,007 villages.

As close confidants of the Nizam, the Paigah nobles enjoyed significant social status. They were given the responsibility of looking after the security and defence of the state.

Abdul Fateh Khan Tegh Jung founded the Paigah nobility and rendered service to the second Nizam, who ruled between 1760 and 1803. He was awarded the title of Shams-ul-Umra, meaning 'the Sun among the masses'. Tegh Jung died in 1786 and is in the Paigah tomb complex. An iron plaque at the entrance of the complex traces the Paigah lineage and exalts the marble magnificence of the vault in which he is buried.

In the medieval era, noted Muslim families had their own graveyards where members of their family would be buried. Shams-ul-Umra's family was laid to rest in the cemetery known as the Paigah tombs.

Some of the Paigah nobles who have been laid to rest here are Asman Jah, Viqar-ul-Umara and Shams-ul-Umara.

As patrons of arts, literature and sports, they were very aesthetically inclined and their family cemetery is a unique specimen of extraordinary artistry.

I had been to Hyderabad before and gone to most of the famous tourist sites, eaten the iconic food and, of course, made the trip to Koh-e Ali, or Ali's mountain, which is a very venerable dargah with what is said to be the hand impression of Ali ibn Abi Talib, the Prophet's son-in-law and fourth Caliph of Islam. I went to these tombs just by chance because of a friend's recommendation and am I glad!

Local people claim that the geometrical patterns and designs of these stunning tombs are only one of its kind and exclusive and cannot be found anywhere in the world.

At the entrance of the Pisal banda suburb in Santosh Nagar, I stopped at a small café and asked for directions, but no one seemed to have any idea. As I was following GPS, I just decided to go deeper into the crowded alley. Soon, I saw a modern grave enclosure with the words Paigah Tombs written on it. I felt a little cheated but I'm not one to give up easily and so I persevered. Just behind the grave enclosure, I saw a white gateway and entered. This is the erstwhile *naubat khana* which was where ceremonial music would be played on drums and guards would be stationed.

I could see many dilapidated graves inside a rectangular enclosure on my right and I entered. There were some graves as new as 2009 and some that were obviously at least a century old. They were in a very dilapidated state, and I recalled various verses which talk of the finality of death and futility of gathering wealth:

Sab thaath pada rah jaavega
Jab laad chalega banjara

All your grandeur will come to nought
When the nomad packs up and leaves

By now, I was sighing so loudly at the sense of desolation in the ruined graves and overgrown grass that I was audible to the ASI caretaker Mr Rahmat who then gave me a conducted tour.

I came out into a courtyard and the beauty of the intricate work on the walls, the small cupolas with Grecian horns on the roof was breathtaking, not just in its delicate beauty, but also in its originality. I had never seen work like this before. I could see limestone trellises, ornamented pillars and roundels on the facade of the tomb. Rahmat, who has been looking after the tombs for many years, proudly told me, 'You won't find such work anywhere in the south or north!'

And how can it be that we talk of a tomb and don't compare it to the Taj Mahal? So of course, this is called the Taj of the South, which I think is a gross injustice because there is no similarity in the architectural style and it is beautiful in its own right.

The Paigah family was ranked second only to the nizam of Hyderabad, with whom they were connected via matrimonial alliances. They were fierce loyalists of the nizam and maintained an army to fight for the nizam.

There is an interesting story related by Harriet Ronken Lynton in her book *Days of the Beloved*.[105] She describes an incident during the Imperial Durbar of 1911 in Delhi, to commemorate the coronation of George V.

A scion of the Paigah family, Major Waliud Dowla, educated in Eton, Sandhurst, and Imperial Cadet College in Dehradun, held the king's commission. He stepped in front of George V and raised his sword in the traditional salute to the monarch. As he walked forward, he saw the Nizam sitting there and repeated the same gesture. He was stripped of his commission but he was unperturbed, for as he said in his defence to the enquiry panel, he was loyal to the king-emperor but the nizam was his sovereign!

The word Paigah, that means pomp and rank in Persian, was a title given by the second Asif Jahi Nizam of Hyderabad to the estate of Nawab Abul Fateh Taig Jung Bahadur. The nawab was also conferred with the title of Shams-ul-Umra, which give the tombs its name.

The first tomb, built here in the eighteenth century, of Makrana marble is that of Shams-ul-Umra or the Sun of the nobles himself. It is delicate and pretty but it's the limestone and stuccowork on the tomb enclosures that are mesmerizing. Twenty-seven members of the Paigah family, including the famous Nawab Sir Vicar-ul-Umra are buried here.

The tombs are all in a row, connected by a beautiful, foliated-arched gallery and ornamented pillars with some of the most spectacular limestone jaalis on the facade of the buildings that I have ever seen.

There are a number of open-to-air double-storey enclosures, mostly holding several tombs inside. Each enclosure has limestone jaalis on the walls and the most exquisite carved teak doors on the entrances. The intricately designed jaalis on the tomb walls, with their unique geometrical and floral patterns, keep one spellbound. Each one is unique. No pattern is repeated whether on the facade or inside. Some of the motifs used are fruits, drums, serpents, flowers and vases.

The crypts themselves are marble with intricately designed *qalams* or takhtis and headstones. A qalam or small raised mound on the cenotaph denotes that the grave belongs to a male and a flat design of a slate denotes that a female is buried there.

The architectural style inside the tombs and galleries is a mix of Greek, Mughal, Rajasthani, Deccani and Persian while the design on the roof is Moorish. It is a beautiful amalgamation that reminds one of the harmonies of God's creation.

The 30-acre compound includes a mosque and prayers are still held here. The sounds of the *azaan* calling the faithful to prayer and the namaz waft over the graves.

One of the most notable tombs is that of Hussain-un-Nissa Begum, daughter of the fifth Nizam who was married to Khursheed Jah. Known for being a replica of Mumtaz Mahal's tomb inside Taj Mahal, this tomb boasts beautiful pietra dura inlay work on Makrana marble. There is also the tomb of Parwarish-un-Nissa, daughter of the fifth Nizam and wife of Nawab Bashir-ud-Daulah, whose tomb is one of the best carved ones in the complex. Extensive jaali work and floral stucco ornamentation capture the vivid imagination of any student of architecture. Ornate wooden doors are made of mahogany, teak and rosewood surviving, almost miraculously, the test of time. One of the most notable tombs is that of Lady Zahir-e-Jung, who died in 1996. She was responsible for handing over the tombs to the Archaeology Department. Another elaborate tomb is that of Fakhruddin Khan, a son-in-law of the second Nizam. There is also an intricately carved tomb of Nawab Zahir Yar Jung, the Last Amir-e Paigah, who died in 1968.

Some photographs taken by Willoughby Wallace Hooper in 1870, now in the J. Paul Getty Collection[106] capture a time when the family must have had resources and means to upkeep it.

I am glad the Paigah family has handed over this architectural marvel to the ASI as part of our national heritage for safekeeping.

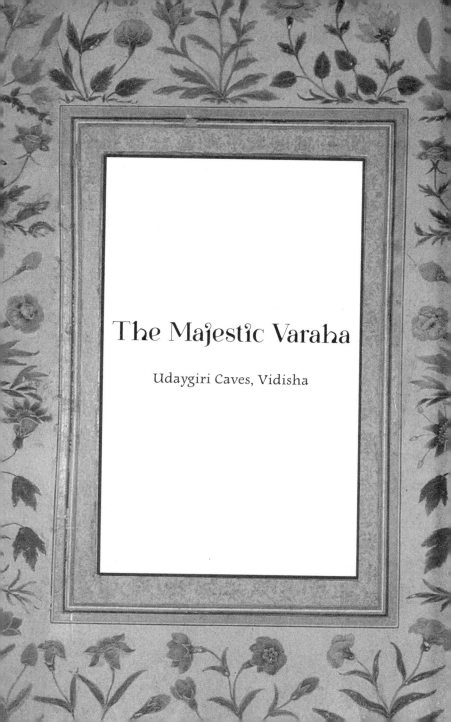

The Majestic Varaha

Udaygiri Caves, Vidisha

Religious architecture forms a major portion of India's built heritage. Apart from being a major source of documenting history, it was also a statement of the local ruler's power.

Just like secular architecture, religious architecture too was bound by its geographical location as material used depended on that. It was also a reflection of the piety of the artisans and workers involved in it. Nothing else can explain the hard work that went into cutting through solid natural rock to carve out temples and spectacular sculptures. Rock-cut architecture never fails to awe me with its sheer majesty and magic.

The earliest rock-cut architecture is from the Mauryan dynasty in third century CE, but Ajanta caves is one of the earliest rock-cut temples.

I close my eyes and imagine the devotion, dedication and skill of the workers chiselling and cutting into solid rock from top to bottom with primitive tools, not much light, completing one section and then starting another. I am sure that the constant chiselling sounded like temple bells to them.

I visited the Ajanta caves a few decades ago and it was a jaw-dropping moment. Udaygiri caves in Vidisha, MP, though not as popular, is a natural progression of the art during the Gupta period (350–550 CE).

These caves were not just an expression of religious piety but also a political statement.

The word Udaygiri means sunrise mountains and I can well imagine how the sun shining on these mountains would have invoked the piety of the people who carved temples here.

The caves lie on two low sandstone hills between the

Udaigiri Caves

rivers Betwa and Bes. It is possible that when these caves were carved out it was directly on the Tropic of Cancer and thus the name that translates to Mount of Sunrise. On the day of the summer solstice, the sun would have been directly overhead, making it a place of worship.

The general direction of the caves is from northwest to southeast, and it reaches to 350 feet, at its highest in the northeast end. The hill has soft white stone, disposed in horizontal layers.

It bears marks of extensive quarrying as this would have been the source of stones and beams for houses in the ancient times.

Two of the caves possess inscriptions of Chandra Gupta II and a third has an inscription dated year 106 of the Gupta Kal (Gupta Age).

The Gupta period was one of political stability and the Gupta rulers personally patronized and encouraged art and architecture. An atmosphere favourable to a revival of all forms of human activity—spiritual and material—was created. It was under the Guptas that we see for the first time, the use of dressed stone masonry, which marked a huge step in the technique of building construction.

Percy Brown writes that, its introduction 'placed a new power in the hands of the workman' and from it emerged the earliest known conception of the Hindu 'house of god'.[107]

The desire for something more positive than spiritual essence and a need for some material interpretation of the religious ideal gave rise to a visible form, usually an idol.

After the conception of an anthropomorphic deity, a structural shrine was a natural progression.

Brown outlines the various stages of Hindu temple architecture from a leafy bower, then a reed hut and afterwards a cella of wood and brick, eventually evolving under the Guptas into a small stone chamber called garbha-griha, literally meaning 'womb-house'. The main deity was kept in this garbha-griha. It was square in plan with plain, dark interiors and richly carved exteriors with a single opening. Some of them would have a pillared portico in front.

Udaygiri has 20 caves, which were numbered by Alexander Cunningham who conducted archeological investigations in 1875. He numbered only 10 caves, probably following the sequence in which they were excavated. That is why cave number one is far away from the rest, on top of a hill. In fact, it is called a false cave since the roof is the natural ledge of the rock in which the side walls and pillars were integrated.

Later studies identified 20 caves, which were numbered separately. Out of these, one cave is dedicated to Jainism and the rest are dedicated to Hinduism.

I first heard of the Udaygiri caves in relation to my research on the Iron Pillar in the Qutub Complex in Delhi. That famous pillar was said to have been brought to Delhi by Sultan Iltutmish from here and indeed there is a depiction of it in the Udaygiri caves.[108] It was supposed to have been fixed here. Another name for Udaygiri was Visnupadagiri (the hill with the footprint of Vishnu) and that is given as the original spot of the Iron Pillar.

This site has iconography related to Vaishnavism, Shaivism and Shaktism (Durga) worship, plus important inscriptions from the Gupta period.

Lord Vishnu is famous for his 10 avatars: Matsya (the Fish), Kurma (the Tortoise), Varaha (the Boar), Narasimha (the Man-Lion), Vamana (the Dwarf), Parasurama (Brahmin warrior), Lord Rama (the Perfect Man), Lord Krishna, Lord Buddha and Kalki.

Of all the caves it is number five that is the most famous,

with its colossal Varaha sculpture and it is here that I went first. It is a large cut in the rock face of the hill, 22 feet in length, 12 feet eight inches in height and three feet four inches in depth.

This iconic relief sculpture represents the story of the rescue of Bhudevi (earth). Hiranayaksh, a demon attacked and kidnaped Goddess Earth and confined her in the cosmic ocean. Vishnu appeared in his boar avatar—Varaha—and rescued her and restored her to her rightful position. She is shown hanging on to his right tusk.

The image of Varaha with his right hand on his knee and left on his hip is impressive in its aggression and power. His left foot treads on the coils of the Naga king, who is guarding the cosmic ocean and has a canopy of 13 snakes' heads, seven in front and six in the intervals behind. His right hand rests on his hip and his left hand is on his knee. It is the most famous and iconic depiction of Lord Vishnu as Varaha.

The depths of the ocean are represented by long undulating lines on the background of the rock to create the waves of the cosmic ocean and are rhythmic and soothing.

On both sides are carved rows of admiring divine figures such as Brahma, Shiva on Nandi and other gods with halos, heavenly musicians, demons, rishis and humans. Another line is occupied by Asurs or demons, flying Devas and a third line by bearded Rishis.

To the right of the Varaha are other sculpted gods and goddesses. Of these, a majestic Durga slaying the buffalo demon Mahishasura, Ganga and Yamuna descending from the heavens and Samudra standing in waves are noteworthy. Ganga is carved standing on a crocodile and Yamuna on a tortoise. The two rivers then join together and enter the sea, where they are received by the god of ocean, who is represented standing in the water above his knees, and holding a water-vessel in his hands.

What seems to be a figure of Chandragupta II is shown kneeling behind the Naga King. It was probably a political metaphor to show that the reason for his conquests was that he represented the Primeval Boar or the Varaha, in defeating chaos and evil. The idea seems to have caught the imagination of the people.

After spending a considerable amount of time in cave number five, I made my way up the hill to the other caves. The original builders took advantage of the horizontal lines of cleavage to excavate numerous caves in the northeast face of the hill. Though many are small in size, originally, they would have had structural porticoes in front.

Cave number six is close to cave number five and is called the Chandragupta Cave. It is a rock-cut sanctum entered through a door and has a simple linga inside and some carvings on the wall outside. These are figures of Vishnu and of Shiva as well and Goddess Durga slaying Mahishasura. A figure of Ganesha is also carved outside the cave. An inscription inside indicates that it was excavated in the reign of Chandragupta II, supervised by Virasena, his minister during 382–401 CE. An image outside, on the outer left side, has a carving of what is popularly believed to be an image of Delhi's Iron Pillar.

It is a short walk from cave five and six and my next stop was cave number eight. It is an almost isolated mass of rock, hewn into the shape of a hemispherical stupa, with a square base. Cave number eight was called the Tawa Cave by Cunningham as it is crowned by a large, flat stone, which resembles a gigantic tawa or griddle, used for baking bread. It is about 14 feet long and 12 feet broad. This cave contains an inscription from the Gupta era that helps date it to fifth century CE.

Another famous cave is cave number four, called the Veena Cave after the figures of two seated veena players carved on its lintel. These veena players have become a little indistinct over the ages and are far more clearly identified in Beglar's photographs of the same from 1875.[109]

The *ekamukha linga* inside it is breathtaking and one of the treasures of the cave complex. The serene face with hair falling on both sides and a carved necklace at the throat make it exquisite.

From here we walk up the hill and there are carvings on the rock face as well as the temples. The notable one here is cave number 13.

Cave number 13 is very fascinating with a magnificent carving of Lord Vishnu sleeping on Adiseshan. This posture of him is called Anantasayanam, meaning sleeping or resting in bliss. There are two men carved below his leg, one larger kneeling devotee in namaste posture and another smaller standing figure behind him. The kneeling figure is said to be Chandragupta II, symbolizing his devotion to Vishnu, while the other is his minister Virasena.

The cave is shallow and the carving is life size, so I had a tough time trying to capture it with my camera, but the image is safe in my head.

Cave number 19, known as the Amrita Cave, is the largest and the scene of the Samudra Manthan (churning of the oceans) is carved on it, resulting in Cunningham calling it Amrita, after the nectar that was produced by this churning of the ocean. The doorway of the cave is much more extensively decorated than the other caves with the pattern of the pilasters outside, resembling the pillars inside. There is a *mukhlingam* inside.

Here too, the two river goddesses are carved on the doorway.

Cave number 20 is dedicated to Jainism and has an image of the Tirthankar Parshvanatha (twenty-third Tirthankar of Jainism) sitting under a serpent hood.

These caves showcase a developed fourth- and fifth-century Hindu iconography and are a must-see for anyone interested in Indian architecture and heritage.

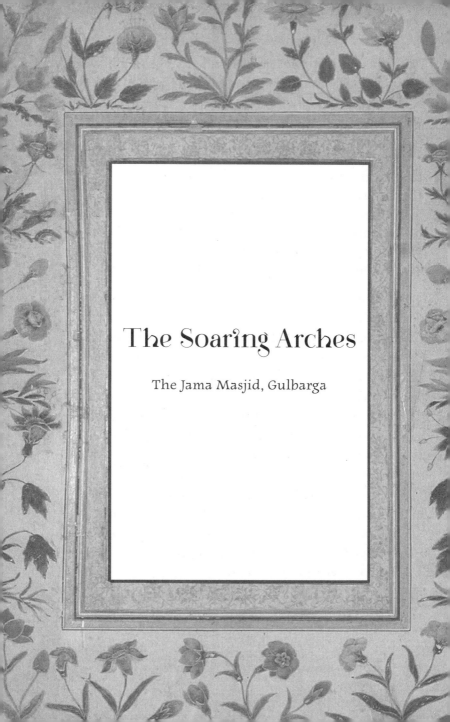

The Soaring Arches

The Jama Masjid, Gulbarga

We had two clear destinations in mind when a friend and I went on a trip to South India without an itinerary. We were quite sure we wanted to visit Hampi and Gulbarga, and decided to work in all the other places of mutual historic interest in between.

Muhammad bin Tughlaq, who reigned between 1321 and 1351 as the Delhi Sultan, had captured large parts of the Deccan that included Gulbarga.

Hasan Gangu was one of his officers who later went on to found the Bahmani Kingdom in the Deccan. A very interesting account of his life is given in *Tarikh-e Firishta*.

Muhammad Qasim Firishta (1560–1620) writes:

Hussun, a native of Dehly, was the servant of Gungoo, a brahminical astrologer, enjoying high favour with the Prince Mahomed Toghluk, and who, in consideration of the good conduct of Hussun, gave him a pair of oxen, and permitted him to till a small piece of land for his own use. While at work one day, the plough attached itself to some substance, which on examination Hussun found to be a chain fastened to a copper vessel, containing a number of antique gold coins. On making the discovery, he carried the treasure to his master, who, commending him for his honesty, acquainted the Prince Mahomed Toghluk with the circumstance, who communicated it to his father, the King. The monarch ordered Hussun to the presence, and conferred on him the command of one hundred horses.[110]

The Brahmin also promised him a life of great distinction. However, this story does not appear anywhere else except in *Tarikh-e Firishta*. It is more probable that he had Persian ancestry and was a descendant of the 'Kokuyads' of Isfahan and the sobriquet was Kanku.[111]

This is not the only anecdote about Hasan's success. Apart from this, another famous anecdote relates to Hazrat Nizamuddin Auliya, who had predicted monarchy for him, when Hasan had visited his khanqah in Delhi as an indigent man.

Many years ago, I was in the dargah of Hazrat Nizamuddin Auliya and was invited to partake in the langar. As it was getting late, I started making excuses. Peerzada Altamash Nizami told me this story and said that anyone who breaks bread here is destined for great things. How could I refuse after that! He then told me this story.

Hazrat Nizamuddin gave instructions to one of his disciples to escort the 'sultan' who was sitting outside his door, into his chamber. The disciple found only one man siittng in tattered clothes. Hazrat Nizamuddin Auliya indicated that he was the guest he was inviting. That man was Hasan Gangu. The Sufi saint opened his fast with a piece of barley bread and shared a piece with Hasan saying that after sharing this bread he was destined to become a sultan. It is said that when Hasan Gangu founded the Bahmani Sultanate, the emblem on his flag was a piece of bread!

In the aftermath of Muhammad bin Tughlaq's disastrous policies, the Deccan became a contentious region and an army was sent to quell the rebellion. Nasiruddin Taghalchi, Ismail Mukh and Hasan Gangu along with a few others had rebelled against the Delhi sultan and captured the citadel of Daulatabad. Ismail Mukh was elected to the throne by them with the title of Abul Fath Nasiruddin Ismail Shah, as the first independent sultan of the Deccan. Hasan Gangu was awarded with the title of Zafar Khan.

Later, after a victory over the Tughlaq forces by Zafar Khan, Abul Fath Nasiruddin Ismail Shah abdicated in favour of Zafar Khan. He ascended the throne in 1347, as Alauddin Hassan Bahmani and established the Bahmani Kingdom (1347–1527), with its capital in Gulbarga, which he made a fortress city. Till the capital was shifted to Bidar, in 1424, the Bahmani sultans ruled from here.

When Muhammad bin Tughlaq shifted his capital to Daulatabad in the Deccan, he brought artisans and architects who made a profound impact on the local architecture.

However, the Bahmani sultans chose to look towards Persia as a source of inspiration (much as Europe did towards Greek architecture) and adopted Persian architectural styles with their lightness of touch and soaring arches. At times it was combined with existing and developing local styles or left unchanged from the Tughlaq style as seen in the tombs of the Bahmani kings in Gulbarga. The Central Asian and Iranian influence that was visible here is 'in part as a response to the growing links with those regions caused by the migration of foreign nobles.'[112]

Initially, mosques in India were built in the hypostyle with aisles around a huge courtyard, with a qibla wall in the aisle facing west. Firuz Shah Tughlaq had mosques with colonnaded aisles around a courtyard (open or covered) with multiple small domes. Under the Lodis and Suris, the prototype of a single/multi-aisled mosque with a courtyard in front was developed. The open courtyard would have the tank for ablution.

The Delhi and provincial sultanates followed many plans.

One of the most striking is the plan of the Gulbarga Jama Masjid.

It had always been my dream to see it, because of its much talked about similarity to the mosque of Cordoba. As we came close, I could see the irregular fortress walls. These measured about three kilometres and were built solidly with 50 feet thick double walls surrounded by a moat carved out of the living rock, in some places 30 yards wide. I could see some solid semicircular bastions as we entered through one of the two entrance gateways of this fort.

I was a little disappointed as I saw the crumbling wall and gateway, with cattle grazing, as I expected more ruins. But the first sight of the grand Jami Masjid or congregational mosque built inside it was enough to set my heart soaring like the arches inside.

The Jami Masjid was completed in 1367 and even now, after 650 years, stands as a firm testimony to the glory of a bygone kingdom. Though I have yet to visit Cordoba, as soon as I entered, I could see why the comparison is made to its Great Mosque.

The uniqueness of the mosque is that it has no open courtyard and the entire structure is covered by a roof. According to the famous art historian Percy Brown,

> Some of the originality of its design and construction may be due to the fact that it was produced under the direction of a hereditary architect named Rafi, not of India, but from the distant town of Kazvin in northern Persia. It is possible that this talented descendant of a noted family of architects evolved the scheme of this mosque from his inner consciousness,

that its unusual conformation was the result of his own genius.[113]

Brown further says that,

he may have looked to the Occident for his inspiration, and that at the back of his mind was some idea of a domed and vaulted hall of the basilica type, an occasional form of Moslem religious edifice in some of the countries of eastern Europe.

The 216-feet-long and 176-feet-wide mosque is divided into wide cloisters with a spacious nave on the west for the mihrab, covered by the high central dome.

Rows of aisles with 68 bays, each roofed over by a cupola, give the pillared hall a magnificent appearance. Honeycomb pendentives on the four sides of each cupola add to this interesting look.

These rows of wide-spanned single arches with low imposts were giving me goosebumps with their perfection and geometrical symmetry. After I prayed in front of the western mihrab I couldn't resist getting myself photographed under every arched bay.

In my excitement, I had plunged straight into the mosque to see its famed arches and so only when I was satiated with that did I come out and see it from the outside. It was one of solid plainness, used to as I was to the one-aisled mosques of Delhi with open courtyards and decorated entrances. Even the lofty arch on the northern entrance was plain without calligraphy.

As the area in front of it was cramped, I got a better view of it from a nearby bastion which houses one of the biggest cannons in the world. From this elevation, I could see the central dome and the four smaller domes on the sides and the arched openings running on three sides of the mosque.

According to Brown, this mosque influenced many other mosques of the Deccan built subsequently, 'the clerestory supporting the dome became a feature of the building art in these parts, while the wide-span and low imposts of the cloister arches figured as the keynote to many of the later monuments,'[114] including the Kali mosque and Khirkee mosque in Delhi. Both these mosques were built in the reign of Firuz Shah Tughlaq.

The building is very plain without any decorative elements on its walls or mihrab and it's this simplicity which adds to the majesty of the design.

It was a design that influenced mosque architecture of Bidar and Bijapur with many using cloister arches with wide spans and low imposts called 'stretched arches'.

Another remarkable feature is the absence of a minaret so closely associated with mosques.

We then walked around to the tower which houses the famous Gulbarga canons. It was from here that I got a bird's-eye view and could appreciate the grandeur and majesty of the mosque.

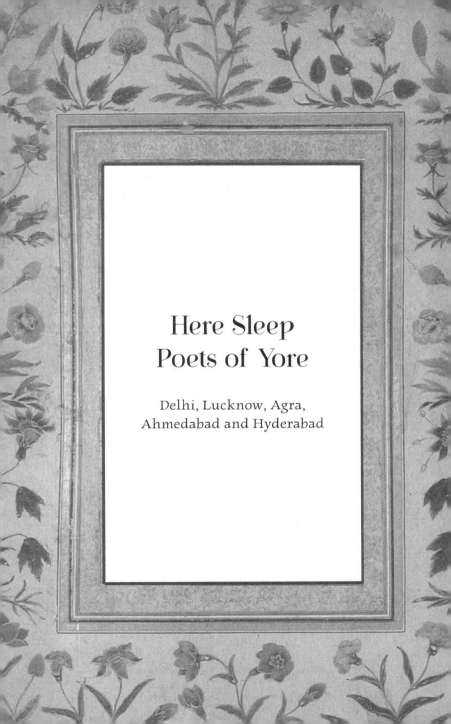

Here Sleep
Poets of Yore

Delhi, Lucknow, Agra,
Ahmedabad and Hyderabad

P oetry has been a way of life in India with many bards composing epics, poems and poetic anthologies from time immemorial. But while we eulogize and remember the poems, we often forget the poets.

I grew up in Lucknow, very close to the place where the Khuda-e Sukhan, or god of (Urdu and Persian) poetry, was supposed to be buried. His grave was lost in the building of the railway station and a small memorial was built nearby. While Urdu poetry has always drawn me to itself, so has the search for the graves of the greats who wrote verses we still recite today or quote as per occasion.

Of course of all these, the grave of Ghalib is well known and has been well looked after too, but for those who read this book and are not from Delhi, please walk down the poetic path with me as I take you to some of the places where these great poets sleep in the three great centres of Urdu poetry—Delhi, Hyderabad, Lucknow, Agra and Ahmedabad.

IN DELHI

Tuti-e-Hind Sheikh Muhammad Ibrahim Zauq's mazaar

Laayi hayaat aaye, qazaa le chalii chale
na apni khushii aaye, na apni khushii chale

Life brought me, death took me away
I neither came of my free will, nor did happiness have
a say

—Zauq

Ustad Sheikh Ibrahim Zauq, as the name invokes, was a master poet and indeed the master of the reigning Mughal emperor Bahadur Shah II whose poetic nom de plume was 'Zafar'.

Zauq was born in 1789, in the house of a soldier living in straitened circumstances. The soldier however, understood the value of a good education and enrolled his son under Hafiz Ghulam Rasool Shauq, who ran a madrasa in their neighbourhood. As the young Ibrahim heard the discussions on poetry in Hafiz Ghulam Rasool Shauq's house, the desire to write awakened in his heart. He started taking guidance from Hafiz ji who suggested the nom de plume of Zauq for him. Later on, he became the student of Shah Naseer and started showing his ghazals to him for improvement.

He also started participating in *mushairas* though lack of patronage was an impediment to his career.

An incident during one of the mushairas disheartened him. He had written a ghazal on the ghazal of the famous Urdu satirist Sauda and took it to Shah Naseer. The latter was offended that his student had the effrontery to write a ghazal on the ghazal of such a famous poet and threw it away.

He came back even more disheartened.

He could not recite it as much as he wanted to, since no master had corrected it. As luck would have it, he met a poet, Mir Kallu Haqeer, with whom he was acquainted. It was Mir who encouraged him to read it in a mushaira to be held and promised to take care of the critics. This gave him much needed encouragement and he soon became very popular.

By then Shah Naseer, who was also the ustad of Prince Abu Zafar Sirajuddin (who later ascended the throne as Bahadur Shah II), had left for the Deccan and he appointed Zauq as his ustad.

When the prince ascended the throne he gave Zauq the title of Khaqani-e-Hind as a reward for a panegyric that he had read in praise of the emperor.

He passed away in 1854 after an illness of 17 days.

In *Waqeat-e Darul Hukumat-e Dehli*,[115] originally published in 1919, Basheeruddin Ahmed describes a famous graveyard near the famous fourteenth-century shrine called Qadam Sharif in Delhi's Paharganj area known as Kallu ka Takiya (Takiya was the dwelling place of a saint) with three trees—imli, peepal and neem—growing in the same spot. Next to it was a small enclosure, which was the last resting place of the Mughal Poet Laureate Sheikh Muhammad Ibrahim Zauq.

Allah ho Akbar
Tuti e Hind Hazrat e Ustad Zauq ne
Li gulshan e jahan se jo bagh jannah ki raah
Saal wafat jo koi pooche to ai Zafar
Kah Zauq jannati za sar bakshish ilaaha

God is Great
The poet laureate Hazrat e Ustad Zauq
Left this worldly garden for the heavenly one
If someone asks his year of death
Say Zauq is a dweller of Paradise, pardoned by God

In Arabic and Persian traditions, chronograms which yield dates via their numerical values are very popular and the emperor himself wrote the chronogram for his master.

At some point after the Partition of India, a public lavatory was made on the spot. This urinal was removed later on court orders after many petitions by Urdu lovers.

Today an enclosure exists with a cenotaph in approximately the same area. Since no one knows where the tombstone or the grave is, the enclosure is called Nishaan-e-Zauq.

The walls of the enclosure have his famous verses inscribed on them.

Though his resting place may be forgotten by lovers of his verses, he has stayed steadfast to his statement:

In dinon garche dakkan mein hai badi qadr-e-sukhan
Kaun jaaye Zauq par Dilli ki galiyan chhod kar

Though these days we hear that poetry is greatly valued in Deccan
But, Zauq, who can leave the alleyways of Delhi

Ghalib's Mazar

Huyi muddat ke Ghalib mar gaya par yaad aataa hai.
Vo har ik baat par kehna, ke, yun hota, to kya hotaa...

It's been a while since Ghalib died but I still remember
His love of argument, and habit of saying if this happened then what?

The famous poet Dabir-ul-Mulk, Najm-ud-Daula Mirza Asadullah Khan Ghalib was born on AD 27 December 1797.

Ghalib needs no introduction. Of all the Urdu poets, he is the most widely read and considered greatest of them all. Sir Muhammad Iqbal equated him with William Shakespeare. His real name is Mirza Asadullah Beig Khan. He started writing verses at the age of 12 and in the beginning his *takhallus* was 'Asad' (lion), which he later changed to 'Ghalib' (conqueror). True to his pen name, he still rules the world with the sheer magic of his poetry. Ghalib is essentially a poet of self-introspection but he was a great thinker and many of his verses reflect some deep philosophical truths. But contrary to the standard practice, he never sent his verses to any senior poet for correction.

His poetry touched a chord in everyone's heart and I doubt there's anyone who has read his verses and can claim that Ghalib didn't speak of his emotions. His poetry was timeless and for all ages.

> *Aate hain ghaib se yeh mazameen khayaal mein,*
> *Ghalib sareer-e-khama nawa-e-sarosh hai.*

From the world unseen come to mind these themes,
Ghalib, the scratching of the pen is the voice of the heavenly angel

Human beings have always run after self-fulfilment, forgetting humanity. This verse of his is as true today as it was then. In fact, more so today, when we glance around and see the crimes and atrocities happening all around us.

> *Bas-ke dushwaar hay, har kaam ka aasan hona*
> *Aadmi ko bhi muyassar nahi, insaan hona*

It is hard for everything to be easy
[as] Man can't even opt to be human

His adult life was spent in impoverished circumstances, fighting for his pension and perpetually in debt, but always with his trademark sense of humour and dignity.

Anecdotes about his wit abound the internet. We owe much to Altaf Husain Hali for writing a beautiful biography of the famous poet Mirza Asadullah Khan Ghalib that describes these vignettes from the poet's life. One such story that comes to mind is about the great poet and his love for a summer fruit.

Come summer and all of us in the subcontinent start thinking of all things mangoes and those abroad start pining for it. Ghalib was extremely fond of mangoes while Hakim Raziuddin Khan, an extremely close friend of Ghalib, didn't like mangoes. One day, both were sitting in Mirza Ghalib's verandah when a donkey driver passed through the lane with his donkey. Some mango skins were lying there; the donkey took a sniff, and then left them.

The Hakim said, 'Look—a mango is such that even a donkey (*gadhaa bhii*) doesn't eat it!'

Ghalib said, 'Without a doubt, only a donkey doesn't eat it.'

Ghalib plays on the word 'Bhii' which means 'too', 'even'.

He died on AD 15 February 1869 and was buried near the Dargah of Hazrat Nizamuddin Auliya in the graveyard belonging to the nawabs of Loharu to whom he was related via his mother and wife's family. It was a very simple grave and only recognizable as the grave of a great poet because of the tombstone with the inscription:

Ya Hayyo Yaa Qayyum
Rashk e Urfi wa fakhr e talib murd
Asadullah Khan Ghalib Murd
Kal main gham o andoh mein ba khatir e mahzoon

Tha turbat e Ustad pe baitha huwa ghamnaak dekha to
mujhe fikr mein tareekh ke, Majruuh Hatif ne kaha ganj
e ma'ni hai tah e khaak

O Living, O Sustaining
The envy of Urfi and the pride of Talib is dead
Asadullah Khan Ghalib is dead
Yesterday I was distraught and grieving
I sat by the grave of my master,
As Majruuh was pondering over a chronogram,
The guardian angel cried 'beneath the dust is a
treasure of meaning'

—Mir Mahdi Majruuh 1285 AH

A marble tomb built by Aga Khan Trust for Culture replaced the old simple grave in 2010.

And seeing the drooping flowers put on his grave I recalled his verse,

Huye mar ke hum jo ruswa, huye kyun na garq-e-darya
Na kabhi janaaza uthta, na kahin mazaar hota

This ignomy after death, why wasn't I drowned in the river
Nor would my coffin be lifted, nowhere my tomb would be

The chronogram for the date of his death is:

Aah Ghalib bamurd

Alas! Ghalib died

Grave of Momin Khan Momin

Momin Khan Momin is one of the greats of Urdu poetry. A contemporary of Ghalib, it is said that Ghalib offered his entire diwan in exchange for one verse.

Tum mere paas hote ho goya
Jab koi doosra nahin hota

You are close to me [as if]
When no one else is

He was born into a family of physicians and he himself
was a practising Hakeem. He also took much interest in
astrology.

One of Delhi's secret is his grave in the compound of the
Sufi saint, Shah Waliullah (1703–1762). Shah Waliullah was
an Islamic scholar, reformer and founder of modern Islamic
thought who attempted to reassess Islamic theology in the
light of modern changes. The area where Shah Waliullah is
buried was called Mehdian and this was the Qabristan-e-
Mehdian.

Since Momin was of a religious bent of mind he was
buried there.

Qabristan-e-Mehdian was once a huge area with the
graves of many saints and ordinary people. Today, much of
it has been taken over and what is left of it is used as a dhobi
ghat. In the 1960s, when Delhi was expanding, there was a
move to bulldoze this area and build flats or bungalows here.
A great lover of Momin, Ali Muhammad, Sher-e-Mewat,
heard of this and came from Mewat (in Haryana) to save
them. It is said that he lay on the road in front of Teen
Murti House and did not get up even when Pandit Nehru
was being driven out in his car. Eventually, Nehruji got down
from his car to enquire and upon hearing the plight of the
graves of Shah Waliullah and Momin Khan Momin he got
the demolition immediately halted. Ali Muhammad, Sher-
e-Mewat, got the mazars repaired and erected a boundary

wall. It is said Ali Mohammed also lay before the bulldozers earlier and suffered a fractured leg. His name is given as Sher Ali Mewati on the internet and also in a book I read but Dr S.Y. Quraishi corrected me, as his ancestors are buried there and he knew about the incident.

Dargah of Mir Dard

Shamaa ki maanind ham is bazm mein
chashm-nam aaye the daaman-tar chale

Like a candle to this gathering
I came with wet eyes, and left with a damp hem

Khwaja Mir Dard (1721–1785), along with Mir Taqi Mir and Mirza Sauda, is considered one of the three major poets of the Delhi School. Mir Taqi Mir, perhaps the greatest of all Urdu poets, acknowledged by Mirza Ghalib, was a poet of love and pathos. Mirza Sauda is remembered for his satire and panegyric. Khwaja Mir Dard, a Sufi saint of the Naqshbandi Majdudi silsilah was a mystic poet. His greatness lay in translating his mysticism into verse.

I went in search of his mazar, and though many people were unaware of its whereabouts, finally an old man told me it was next to Zakir Hussain College. The entrance to the Khwaja Mir Dard Basti, an urban slum (adjacent to Zakir Hussain College) that has been named in the poet's honour, also houses the tomb.

The mazar is inside the basti and is a shabby circular building made of bricks with a tin roof.

There are 13 graves inside with the poet's grave on the left corner.

These graves include that of Mir Dard's grandson Khwaja Nasir Wazir Andaleeb and his younger brother Khwaja Muhammad Mir Asar.

Once upon a time, it was in a small orchard named after the poet. The peeling paint, the dirty, dusty graves bear mute testimony to our neglect of our icons.

This is the tomb of someone who is considered the greatest mystic poet of Urdu. Maybe his pen name, Dard, was prophetic. Because I certainly was very pained.

IN HYDERABAD

Grave of Dagh Dehlvi

Nawab Mirza Khan, popularly known as Dagh Dehlvi, is famous for his Urdu ghazals. Unfortunately, after the fall of the Mughal Empire he had to leave Delhi for Rampur where Nawab Yusuf Ali Khan welcomed him.

In 1888, he left for Hyderabad. Here he became the court poet and mentor of the sixth nizam Mir Mahbub Ali Khan who gave him the title of Dabeer ud Dawla, Faseeh ul Mulk, Nawab Nizam Jang Bahadur, Sipah Salar, Yar-e-Wafadar, Muqrib-us-Sultan, Bulbul-e-Hindustan, Jahan Ustad, Nazim Yar Jung.

He died here on 17 March 1905 and was buried in the Yousufain Dargah. His wife had preceded him and their graves are close to each other.

I had to hunt for it because I didn't know where it was but it's fairly easy to locate on the right-hand edge of the courtyard.

Grave of Mahlaqa Bai Chanda

On my numerous visits to Hyderabad, I have always walked up the 500 steps, sometimes barefoot, to pray for strength to overcome difficulties or offer prayers of gratitude once fulfilled, at the shrine known simply as Koh-e-Ali or Maula Ali ka Pahad (the Hill of My Lord Ali). I am not alone, as lakhs visit this shrine every year. Ali ibn Abi Talib, the fourth Caliph of Islam and the first Imam of the Shia sect is called Mushkil Kusha or solver of difficulties.

According to *Tuzuk-e-Qutub Shahi*, a eunuch in the court of Ibrahim Qutb Shah IV, dreamt that a man dressed in green told him to visit a hill where Maula Ali was waiting for him. In his dream, the eunuch went there and found Maula Ali waiting for him on top of the hill with his hand resting on a stone. The next day he saw a stone with an imprint of a hand on the hill. He got it hewn out of the rock and built a masonry arch over it.

On hearing about it, Sultan Ibrahim Qutb Shah (1550–80) visited it and ordered a mosque to be built there. Since then that entire area was known as Koh-e-Ali. The rock with the hand imprint is enshrined at the back of the dargah and kept covered by a cloth and flowers and is said to have healing powers.

This year on my visit to Koh-e-Ali, I went in search of another devotee of Maula Ali whose devotion was so deep that she, a poet, ended nearly every verse with Ali's name and is buried near the foot of it. She had replaced the existing wooden canopy on the shrine and had gotten a marble one made in its place.

O Venus, your night brings a wounded heart no rest
Only sighing, complaining and crying becomes his
day
Only if Chanda passes each breath remembering
Ali's name
Does her life count and the passing time becomes a
day

(translation: Scott Kugle)[116]

Her name was Chanda (moon) and Asaf Jah II, nizam of Hyderabad gave her the title Mahlaqa Bai (moon-faced lady). She was born in 1768 to Mida Bai aka Roop Kanwar Bai.

Her birth was a miracle as her mother suffered a miscarriage when on a pilgrimage to Koh-e-Ali. Scholar and sage, Shah Tajalli Ali, who was accompanying her, immediately brought her a thread and some incense sticks from the shrine. He tied the thread on her wrist and waved the incense under her nose. Roop Kanwar's bleeding stopped and the foetus was saved.

Chanda Bibi went on to become one of the most important courtesans of the court of Asaf Jah II Nizam Ali Khan. She was extremely accomplished. The renowned exponent of khyaal and dhrupad singing, Khush-hal Khan was her teacher. She was also proficient at warfare as well as at being a consummate politician. She not only patronized poets and people of letters, she rode to war with the Nizam dressed in male clothes.

Though she may not be the first woman to have her diwan published as popularly believed, she is the first to give Urdu poetry a feminine voice.

Faiyaz Wajeeh, a journalist, tells me that the credit of

being the first woman to have a diwan published goes to Lutfun-Nisa of Bijapur, whose diwan (original is in Salar Jung Museum) came out a year before in 1797. The reason why Lutfun-Nisa is overlooked is because she wrote under a male sounding pen name of Imteyaz.

In 1792–93 when her mother passed away, Mahlaqa Bai got a tomb made for her at the foot of Koh-e-Ali.

She herself was buried next to her mother in 1824. A plaque on the gateway of her tomb reads:

> Cypress of the garden of grace and rose tree of the grove of coquetry
> An ardent inamorata of Haider and supplicant of Panjetan
> When the glad tidings of the advent of death arrived from God
> She accepted it with her heart and heaven became her abode
> The voice of the invisible speaker called for her chronogram
> Alas! Mahlaqa of the Deccan departed for heaven
> 1240 AH (AD 1824)

Over the years, the garden went into disuse and no one knew that it was the resting place of a woman, whom the Nizam had given the rank of an umara and whose palanquin was preceded by drummers and 500 armed guards.

As I wandered in the now beautiful garden tomb and recited fatiha on her grave, I blessed Scott Kugle, a professor of Emory University who researched the life of Mah Laqa Bai and deduced that this dilapidated garden was her tomb.

With the help of funds from the US Ambassador's Fund

for Cultural Preservation, it was renovated with supervision by the Centre for Deccan Studies.

IN LUCKNOW

Grave of Mirza Muhammad Rafi Sauda

Mirza Muhammad Rafi Sauda (1713–1781) is one of Urdu's greatest satirist. He was born in Shahjahanabad (present-day Old Delhi) but migrated first to Farrukhabad to the court of the nawabs of Bangash where he lived from 1757 to about 1770 and then to Lucknow, to the court of the nawab of Awadh, where he died.

He had written a *shahr ashob*, a genre of Urdu poetry, for Delhi after the sacking of Delhi by the Perisan king Nadir Shah in 1739.

Muhammad Rafi Sauda writes after Nadir Shah's invasion:

Jahanabad tu kab iss sitam ke qabil tha
Magar kabho kisi aashiq ka yeh nagar dil tha
Ke yun mita diya goya ke naqsh-e-batil tha
Ajab tarah se yeh bahr-e-jahan mein sahil tha
Ke jis ki khaak se leti thi falak moti rol

[Shah] jahanabad you were never deserving of such tyranny
You were once the heart of lovers, many.
Why has it been destroyed as if a lie by destiny?
T'was a wondrous beach in the sea of plenty
Precious stones on your shores galore.

A chance remark by a friend led me in search of Mirza Rafi Sauda's grave. I found his simple grave in the Imambara of

Agha Baqar in Old Lucknow. The imambara itself is the second oldest in Lucknow and dedicated to Hazrat Abbas, the son of Hazrat Ali, the fourth Caliph of Islam and the first Shia Imam.

The imambara is a pretty, white and green structure with delicate minarets and three domes, decorated with stucco ornamentation in the Lucknow style. The interior has been modernized with glass mosaic patterns but the exterior remains old.

There is a large courtyard with graves; as it was considered auspicious to be buried in a religious structure, we find dargahs and imambaras full of gravestones.

There is just a marble tombstone on the floor amongst many others which indicates where the great poet is buried.

Mir Annes ka Maqbara
Credit: Arsh Ali

Mir Anees's Mazar

Umr guzri hai isi dasht ki sayyahi main
Paanchvi pusht hai Shabbir ki maddahi main

I've spent a lifetime traversing this desert with
veneration
In Shabbir's service I am the fifth generation

I grew up hearing Mir Anees's *marsiyas* and on a recent visit
to Lucknow, I decided to read the fatiha on his grave. The
rickshaw took me into a narrow alley near Lucknow's Akbari
Darwaza. From there, I negotiated my way through the dirt
and slush that cover most alleys in old areas of India. I reached
what was once a grand doorway and saw that some steps
led to a locked iron grill. After enquiry, a family nearby said
that the keys were with a family member of Mir Anees. He
kindly led me to his house through more narrow alleys and
a family member accompanied us back.

The grave building was clean, though the grounds were
overgrown.

Mir Babar Ali Anees was born in Faizabad in 1803 to
Mir Khaleeq, a marsiya writer. As was normal in those days,
he received a comprehensive education which included Arabic
and Persian literature, horse riding, fencing, etc. Spending his
childhood in Ayodhya meant that he was steeped in Awadhi
culture and Indian traditions.

With 22 poets in his family it was but natural that by
the time he was 13 he was writing ghazals and later six-line
marsiyas. Initially his father was his ustad and he suggested
that the young Anis concentrate on marsiya. After shifting
to Lucknow he came under the tutelage of the famous

Lucknow poet, Imam Baksh Nasikh.

The word marsiya is derived from the Arabic word *Risa*, meaning a great tragedy or lamentation for a departed soul. It is an elegy, a poem of mourning which has now come to be specifically associated with the tragedy of Karbala and to describe the battle fought on the plains of Karbala in Iraq by Hazarat Imam Husain and his supporters against the army of Yazid.

Yazid, the second Caliph of the Umayyad dynasty, was widely accepted by both Shias and Sunnis as being amoral, debauched and a tyrant. Considering it a betrayal of the basic tenets of Islam, and of all that his grandfather, the Prophet, stood for, Imam Hussain had refused to accept Yazid's suzerainty. He preferred to leave Medina for Kufa in Iraq where some friends had invited him, in order to avoid bloodshed. Those friends eventually buckled down under Yazid's oppression. Hussain had already travelled a distance when he came to know of it. He was confronted by Yezid's considerable army on the dusty plains of Karbala and forced to camp there. On AD 10 October 680/10th of Muharram 60 AH, the first month of the Islamic calendar, Hussain was martyred in battle alongside all the male members of his family, except one son who was too ill to fight.

This act of supreme sacrifice, acceptance of certain martyrdom of self and family, with knowledge of untold and intense suffering awaiting the surviving women and children of his family, yet steadfast refusal to compromise the principles of his grandfather, became the incomparable metaphor for truth and integrity.

Marsiyago pay tribute to this martyrdom. This form of poetic genre flourished in Awadh under the Persian origin

Shia nawabs till it reached a literary zenith. Today one cannot conceive of the observance of Muharram without a marsiya.

Marsiya generally consists of six-line units, with a rhyming quatrain and a couplet on a different rhyme.

It is characterized by six-line verses in an AA, AA and BB rhyme scheme. They are traditionally either recited by Marsiya-Khwans or sung by a Marsiya-Soz.

Lucknow had several marsiyagos but none as famous and sublime as Mir Anees who combined the Arabic classical poetic traditions with the local Awadhi culture. He created tragic scenes of loss and desolation of the women after the martyrdom of Imam Hussain and the men, conjuring vivid battle scenes, and made each heroic character come live before our eyes.

Shamsur Rahman Faruqi, famous Urdu critic and scholar writes, 'Mir Anee's marsiyas are the best pre-modern model in Urdu of narrative-historical, narrative-lyrical and oral-dramatic poetry.'[117]

Mir Anees wrote over 213 marsiyas and other verses commemorating Imam Hussain's martyrdom. He was also a master in the art of writing *rubayi* or quatrain. He could have been as famous as Ghalib had he written ghazals instead of sticking to a specific genre.

He died in 1874 at the age of 72 and was buried in a land he had bought earlier as his family graveyard.

IN AHMEDABAD

Grave of Maulana Naziri Nishapuri

In the course of my wanderings in Ahmedabad I also found the grave of Maulana Naziri Nishapuri, a famous Persian poet who lived during the reign of Akbar.

Naziri Nishapuri (1516–1612/14) was born in Nishapur in Persia and travelled to India and joined the court of another poet Abdur Rahim Khan-e-Khanan.

He is buried in the dargah of Hazrat Kamal Posh in the old city, next to the saint himself. The locality is very crowded. A brand new mosque has been built there, with the graves behind it on the side. I document it here just so that it is recorded.

Prashant Keshavmurthy, professor of Persian literature at the Institute of Islamic Studies, McGill, kindly sent me some notes[118] on his poetic ability.

He wrote that when

> Mirza Bedil Dihlavi (d. 1720) composed a bayāz comprised almost entirely of ghazal chains, each chain comprising ghazals in the same meter and rhyme. But what's interesting is that he was indifferent to the chronological sequence in which poets lived. Instead, he arranged the ghazals beginning with what he considered the best ghazal and followed it with ghazals in order of poetic merit—that is, according to what he considered the most accomplished renditions of poetic themes. In this sense, this anthology lets us infer Bedil's criteria of poetic accomplishment.

At least two such chains begin with ghazals by Naziri and include, as part of ghazals in the same meter and rhyme, ghazals by Bedil himself as well as by Sa'eb-e Tabrizi (d. 1676) and Ghani Kashmiri (d. 1669) and at least one begins with a ghazal by Makhfi—presumably Zeb un-Nisa Makhfi—and includes a ghazal by Naziri.

A few ghazal distichs by Naziri translated by him:

Ze bī-dād-e tu harf-e mehr rā nām u nishān gum shud
Kitāb-e husn rā juzv-e muhabbat az miyān kam shud

By your tyranny is the mention of mercy missing all signs.
Beauty's book is missing the chapter on love.

Chun abr-e bahārī be saram sāya-fagan shud
Bar har bar u būmam ke nazar kard chaman shud

When spring's cloud cast me in its shade
wherever it planted its gaze my countries and
continents burst each into verdure.

Bar khāk-e darash jā-ye shahīdān nadahad kas
Lutfīst ke kāfūr tan o 'itr kafan shud

No room for martyrs at his door.
It's kindness enough that the body
is camphor
and the winding sheet
incense.

IN AGRA

*Tuk hirs-o-hawa ko chhod miyan mat des bides phire
mara*
qazzaq ajal ka lute hai din raat baja kar naqqara
*kya badhiya bhainsa bail shutur kya gu mein palla sar-
bhaara*
*kya gehun chanwal moth matar kya aag dhuan aur
angara*
sab thath pada rah jawega jab lad chalega banjara

O man, discard your greed and desires, wander not in
faraway lands,
The thief of destiny blows his trumpet to loot you day
and night,
Whether buffaloes, bulls, camels and your soiled bags
Bags of wheat, rice, pulses or fire and smoke
All your grandeur will come to nought when the
nomad packs up and leaves

—Nazeer Akbarabadi

This verse from the famous poem 'Banjara-nama (Song
of a Nomad)' has been one of my favourites ever since I
remember. It encapsulates the philosophy of life: travel lightly
for this world is but a place of transit on the way to the
eventual destination which is afterlife.

In a direct contrast to Mirza Ghalib who came from Agra
to Delhi, Nazeer Akbarabadi (1735–1830) was born in Delhi
and migrated with his parents as a child to Agra, hence the
takhallus Akbarabadi (the Mughal name for Agra). His birth
name was Wali Muhammad and he belonged to a prosperous

Syed family. He was born after 12 daughters and his birth was a cause of great celebration. In 1739, after Delhi was devastated by the raid of Nadir Shah the Persian king, the city fell on bad days and his family shifted to Agra, where he received his education. He became a teacher in Mathura and refused to leave that profession though, allegedly, he was given lucrative offers by the Raja of Bharatpur and later the Nawab of Awadh.[119]

A contemporary of famous Rekhta poets Mir Taqi Mir, Muhammad Rafi Sauda, Mirza Ghalib and Momin Khan Momin, Nazeer chose to write about everyday life. Unlike his contemporaries, he is more famous for his nazms, which reflect his moral and didactic principles. Using local and rural idioms he wrote prolificly. Though the major corpus of his work has not survived Khan-e-Khanan we have a 900-page kulliyat or collected works which were published by Nawal Kishore Press.

He died at the ripe old age of 98. He used his time to study human nature and leave behind a legacy of moral and earthy poems which span across human emotions and man-made boundaries. He 'rose above narrow religious and sectarian boundaries to compose a large number of works in different genres of Urdu poetry.'[120]

Raziuddin Aquil adds that Nazeer's kulliyat

offers significant insight into the celebration of the little pleasures of life—fairs, festivals, a fresh burst of energy with the season changing for the better, natural bounties such as juicy summer fruits, some love as well as a chance or opportunity to inteact with women in a regressive society, in wedding parties, alongwith other possibilities of fun.[121]

As someone who studies architecture and writes about it, the dismal condition of tombs often elicits the hook line of 'Banjaranama' for me.

That it would fit in so aptly with the writer of this poem was not something I had anticipated.

The poet's exact birthday is uncertain but locals believe it to be during basant; a local, who has a shop nearby, told me that when Agra was rocked by communal riots sometime in the 1940s, it was to the people's poet who had sung in praise of Eid, Bakreid, Shab-e-Barat, Holi, Diwali and Dussehra that they returned. His birthday celebrations were linked to Basant Panchami. To date, the celebrations start from his grave.

However, his grave, 100 metres from the Taj Mahal in Tajganj's Malko Nagar, is in a pitiable condition.

Housed under a tin shed, the area was muddy and dirty and seemed uncared for.

The poet who wrote the 'Aadmi Nama', and was hailed as the people's poet, has been forgotten by the people.

Achchha bhi aadmi hi kahta hai ai Nazeer
Aur sab mein jo bura hai so hai wo bhi aadmi

It is humans who speaks [and does] good things
O Nazeer
And the one who who does bad, that is also a human.

Acknowledgements

Shauq-e-safar be-sabab aur safar be-talab
Us kii taraf chal diye jis ne pukaaraa na thaa

The desire to travel, spontaneous and the journey
unsought
I left for those places, which had never called me

—Shahzad Ahmad

Ever since I remember, whenever we were asked to list down our hobbies I would write reading and travelling, little knowing that this may become my vocation one day.

When visiting Europe 2010 onwards, I realized that there was a dearth of user-friendly information for travellers who wanted more than just superficial exploration. So I started travel-blogging, giving tips on the best destinations, especially the lesser-known, and the best way to get to them, how to sightsee with the minimum expense. In Europe, since expense is a major concern for tourists, I gave tips on train fares, combination tips for museums, etc.

In 2013, I decided to return to India from the Middle East and settle down in Delhi. I had already started writing on Delhi and was now writing a book. That the one book became a trilogy named *Where Stones Speak* is a matter of destiny.

After the trilogy was completed and I had spent a number of years exploring Delhi, I wanted to go out further. Though we had lived in various parts of India from Kolkata to Kochi, before we left for the Middle East, I realized India, with its vast architectural heritage, was waiting to be explored.

It was around this time in 2016 that I met Mini Kapoor, Ideas Editor, *The Hindu*. She offered me a column in *The Hindu* on my travels and I titled it 'Where Stones Speak'.

So I set off on my explorations, sometimes with friends but mostly alone.

In the two years that I wrote the column I received very encouraging feedback and mail. I was told my columns were being used as reference by UPSC aspirants and coaching classes, and were being enjoyed by armchair travellers and history buffs. It was a wonderful feeling. I would thus like to start off by thanking Mini for this break and *The Hindu* for showcasing the column brilliantly on the centre page.

These columns were brilliantly edited by Radhika Santhanam and my grateful thanks to her for helping me hone my craft.

In 2018, I visited Agra and wrote a column not on the Taj Mahal but a lesser-known tomb of a European officer often called the Red Taj Mahal. Yamini Chowdhury of Rupa Publications read that piece and contacted me for a book on this theme. Thus, this book came into being. Thank you Yamini, I have really enjoyed this journey. A book needs a good editor and I was blessed to have Saswati Bora by my side. I am grateful to Oorja Mishra, the copyeditor,

Rajkumari John for the layout, Rachita Rakyan for the stunning cover and Amit Pasricha for the image.

There are many people I need to thank who have been my travel companions.

My husband who travelled all over Europe with me, getting tired of my obsession with museums and castles, but still keeping pace!

My children who were worried about my solo travels and kept checking on me but encouraged me to fly.

My friend Anuradha Shankar, ADG Bhopal, because of whose help I travelled extensively in Madhya Pradesh, has been a huge support in my journey.

I met a soulmate in Alka Kaushik with whom I travelled in the Deccan. Among the many journeys we travelled together, the most memorable is when we set off with a one-way ticket, intending to return after we had explored to our heart's content.

I hope I can continue travelling for the rest of my life for there is so much more to see and so much more to write about!

'Travelling—it leaves you speechless, then turns you into a storyteller.'

—Ibn Battuta, *The Travels of Ibn Battuta*

Travel Advice

First of all, remember to check the ASI holidays before setting off, especially if you have time constraints. While many of the Indian monuments under the ASI are closed on Mondays, some are closed on Fridays. So, that should be the first point to check. If you are travelling to unfamiliar places by road, make sure you hire reliable taxi services. The various tourist sites on the net will give you reviews and you can get recommendations from services you have used elsewhere and have been happy with.

Hotel accommodation is about budget but as a solo woman traveller I ensure that the places I stay in are secure and within city limits. Once again I go on personal and internet recommendations.

Depending on when you travel, winters being the best time, carry appropriate clothing. In places of worship, ensure that you are wearing clothes which cover the knees for men and body for women. I would advise women to always keep a scarf in their bag in case they see a temple, mosque or dargah they want to visit.

Hire accredited ASI guides only. Even though I do my research before travelling, if I am alone I hire a guide because in case of forts there are some very lonely stretches.

I am not adding timings as these can vary depending on the time of travel. As a thumb rule, ASI monuments are open from sunrise to sunset but it's always better to check.

Agra: It is on the tourist map and very well connected with Delhi by train, flight and road. Hotels of all price ranges are available and one can stay as per their convenience. The Red Taj Mahal is in the Roman catholic Cemetery in the area known locally as Padritola.

A rickshaw or taxi can be hired locally, but even though it is under the ASI its timings isn't governed by their rules. There is no ticket and it is looked after by the cemetery staff.

Address: Padritola, Nehru Nagar, Civil Lines, Agra 282002.

Abhaneri: The nearest airport is Jaipur which is 165 kilometres away, one can hire a car and drive from there. The distance between Delhi and Alwar is 189 kilometres via the eastern periphery and one can go from here by road. The baori is governed by ASI rules of sunrise to sunset timings and remains closed on Mondays. There are also trains between Delhi and Alwar. It takes approximately an hour and a half from Alwar city to the baori.

There are decent hotels if you want stay there as Alwar city, with its Moosa Rani ki Chatri and State Museum, is worth a visit. The imposing Alwar Fort is another half day's exploration.

It is an ASI monument and governed by its rules. It is not a ticketed monument.

Address: Near Harshat Mata Temple, Abhaneri, Dausa, Bandikui, Rajasthan 303313.

Barabar Caves: The nearest city is Gaya which is well connected by air, train and roads. One can stay in Gaya or Bodh Gaya and visit the Mahabodhi Temple and hire a car for Barabar Caves. It is a full-day journey to Barabar and it is advisable to contact the ASI office there and hire a guide. The caves are kept locked to prevent vandalism and the ASI guide will ensure that they are opened. It is a steep walk up the hill, so wear good walking shoes. If you have time, plan in such a way that you keep a day for a visit to Rajgir and Nalanda also. Bodh Gaya has excellent hotels and they arrange for taxis.

It is an ASI monument and governed by its rules. It is not a ticketed monument.

The hills are open and one can see the caves from outside but the interior of the caves are opened only with prior arrangement.

Address: Barabar Hill Road, Barabar, Sultanpur, Bihar 804405.

Burhanpur: The nearest airport is in Indore which is 163 kilometres away. It is connected by train from Delhi and Mumbai. There are comfortable hotels, but not in the luxury range. Burhanpur has a treasure of architectural heritage, including the Asirgarh Fort so do plan for a few days.

It is an ASI monument and governed by its rules. It is not a ticketed monument.

Address: Ahukhana, Zainabad, East Nimar District, Madhya Pradesh 450331.

Champaner: The nearest airport is 49 kilometres away at Vadodara. Ahmedabad is 146 kilometres away. Both these cities are also connected by train and one can make either the base and travel by road from there. Both have good hotels. Please ask your guide to take you to Nagina and Kevda mosques, which are deep inside the city.

They are ASI monuments and are governed by its rules. They are not ticketed monuments.

Address: Jepura, Gujarat 389360.

Chanderi: The nearest airport is Gwalior, which is 146 kilometres away. Lalitpur is the nearest railway station and is around 36 kilometres from Chanderi. This is on the route of major trains. One can find good budget hotels here. Alternatively, this trip can be combined with the heritage rich cities of Orchha and Jhansi and can be reached by road from either of the two. Ask for directions near Badal Mahal. The parisar is located in a residential area and is not easily visible.

Address: Isagarh, Chanderi Rd, Chanderi, Madhya Pradesh 473446.

Daulatabad: The base city for Daulatabad will be Aurangabad which is well connected by air and road. It has good hotels. Your hotel can arrange a taxi for you. It is 16 kilometres away from the city. It is a full-day trip and a very strenuous walk in the fort, so go wearing sturdy walking shoes and carry water. You should hire the ASI guide there. Also, plan in such a way that you have a full day for the Ellora caves and another for Ajanta. For those interested in Sufism, they can visit Khuldabad which has the shrines of many Sufi saints.

It is an ASI monument and governed by its rules. It is a ticketed monument

Address: MH SH 22, Daulatabad, Maharashtra 431002.

Delhi: Delhi is well connected by road, air and train. One can get hotels of all budgets. Turkman Gate in Old Delhi is the point for reaching the grave of Sultan Raziya. From there you can hire a rickshaw or e-rickshaw to Bulbulikhana. The last stretch has to be done on foot. There is a functioning mosque in the premises so please dress accordingly. Also avoid prayer times as you will not be allowed entry.

Address: Bulbulikhana, Turkman Gate, Chandni Chowk, Delhi 110006.

Gulbarga: The nearest airport is in Hyderabad which is around 230 kilometres away and is accessible by road. There are many trains running on this route and it is well connected to all major cities. There are many budget hotels here. The mosque is inside the Gulbarga Fort and can be accessed on all days except Saturday. However, it is a functioning mosque so avoid prayer times and go dressed appropriately.

It remains closed on Saturdays.

Address: Gulbarga Fort, Gulbarga, Karnataka 585101.

Hyderabad: Hyderabad is well connected by air and train and hotels are available for every budget. The Paigah tombs is not a ticketed monument

Address: Qalander Nagar Rd, Santosh Nagar, Kanchan Bagh, Hyderabad, Telangana 500058.

Junagarh: The closest airport is 106 kilometres away at Rajkot. It is connected by train and road.

The maqbaras themselves are kept locked but one can enter the compound. The keys to the maqbara are kept in the mosque nearby and one can go and request them. But it is as per their convenience. Budget hotels are available.

If one plans a road trip, it can be combined with a trip to Dwarka, Somnath and Gir Forest.

Address: Mullawada, Junagadh, Gujarat 362001.

Kalinjar: The nearest airport is at Khajuraho, which is 130 kilometres away. The nearest railway station is Banda, 60 kilometres away. There is a smaller station Atarra, which is 41 kilometres away but isn't so well connected to major cities.

It is easily accessible by road and major towns nearby are Khajuraho and Chitrakoot. Since Khajuraho is a major destination for tourists, this can be combined with that visit.

Address: Kalinjar Fort, Banda District, Kalinjar, Uttar Pradesh 210129.

Kanpur: Kanpur is easily accessible by air, road and train. It has hotels in all price ranges. One has to go by road to the Bhitargaon temple. It is around 50 kilometres from Kanpur. One can also plan a trip from Lucknow, which is a major tourist destination. Plan a full-day trip and include a trip to Bithoor on the Ganges, with its scenic ghats and ashrams and a museum with some fine objects related to Rani Laxmibai, whose birthplace this was and the First War of Indian Independence, 1857.

Address: Bhitargaon, Uttar Pradesh 209214.

Lucknow: It is well connected by air, road and train. Hotels are available under all price ranges.

Mir Anis Maqbara: It is kept locked and one has to request the family staying near the premises to help get the keys.

Address: Near Akbari Gate, Chowk, Lucknow, Uttar Pradesh 226003.

Imambara Agha Baqar: The imambara is a functioning one so please dress appropriately.

Address: Raja Bazar, Yahiyaganj, Lucknow, Uttar Pradesh 226003.

Pandua: The nearest airport is Kolkata. From here there is a good train service. One can stay in Malda which has budget hotels and thus access monuments in both Gaur and Pandua. Make sure you make a plan for at least two to three days.

Address: Adina Mosque, Pandua Road, Pandua, West Bengal 732102.

Rohtas: The nearest airport is in Gaya which is around 185 kilometres away. The nearest big town is Sasaram which is around 90 kilometres away. Both towns are well connected by train and road and from there one can hire a four-wheel drive to Rohtasgarh Fort. One can go up only in a four-wheel drive so please remember that. Wear very sturdy shoes and carry food and water. There is a village with some small shops on the hill, but please go prepared.

Address: Rohtas, Bihar 821311.

Srinagar: It is connected by air. One can travel by road too but there are no trains.

Pari Mahal: It is a ticketed monument and one can hire a taxi/car to go there.

Address: Pari Mahal, Srinagar, Jammu and Kashmir 190001.

Akhund Shah ki Masjid:

Address: Hari Parbat, Nohata, Srinagar, Jammu and Kashmir 190003.

Thanesar: The nearest airport is Chandigarh. There is a train station in the city. It is well connected by road and is around four hours away from Delhi. There are plenty of signboards to take one to the tomb complex. Wear comfortable shoes for the Harsh ka Tila excavation site.

Address: Bari Mohalla, Thanesar, Kurukshetra City, Haryana.

Vidisha: The nearest airport and train station is Bhopal. It is at a distance of 60 kilometres from there. Vidisha is well connected by trains. It is 15 kilometres from Sanchi. One can make a combined trip and both places have decent hotels. Bhimbeteka, the famous rock shelters, are 97 kilometres away from Sanchi.

Address: 35, Nagar Palika Station Road, Swarnkar Colony, Baripura, Vidisha, Madhya Pradesh 464001.

Notes

1. Qaiser, A.J. *Building Construction in Mughal India: Evidence from Painting*, Oxford University Press, 1989.
2. Parihar, Subhash. *Mughal Monuments in the Punjab and Haryana*, Inter India Publications, 1985.
3. Koch, Ebba. *The Complete Taj Mahal*, Thames and Hudson, 2006.
4. Ibid.
5. Khan, M. Abid Ali. *Memoirs of Gaur and Pandua*, ASI, Bengal Secretariat, Calcutta, 1931.
6. Khan, M. Abid Ali. *Short Notes on the Ancient Monuments of Gaur and Panduah*, Malda, 1913.
7. British Library Online Gallery, http://www.bl.uk/onlinegallery/onlineex/apac/addorimss/t/019addor0004883u00000000. html.
8. Ibid.
9. Eaton, Richard M. *The Rise of Islam & the Bengal Frontier 1204–1760*, University of California Press, 1996.
10. Michelle, George. *The Islamic Heritage of Bengal*, UNESCO, 1984.
11. *Gazetteer of the Bombay Presidency, Vol. III*, Government Central Press, Bombay, 1879; The Gazetteer quotes *Mirat-e Sikandari* written in 1611.
12. Ibid.

13. Ibid.

14. British Library Online Gallery, http://www.bl.uk/onlinegallery/onlineex/apac/photocoll/e/019pho0001000s7u00822000.html.

15. British Library Online Gallery. http://www.bl.uk/onlinegallery/onlineex/apac/photocoll/g/019pho001000s18u01863000.html

16. British Gallery Online Library, http://www.bl.uk/onlinegallery/onlineex/apac/photocoll/r/019pho001000s18u01864000.html

17. Asher, Catherine. *Architecture of Mughal India (The New Cambridge History of India)*, Cambridge University Press, 1992.

18. Emperor Jahangir, *Tuzuk-e-Jahangiri*, edited by Henry Beverudge, translated by Alexander Roger, *Project Gutenberg*, https://www.gutenberg.org/cache/epub/53674/pg53674-images.html.

19. Ibid.

20. Safvi, Rana. 'Peace and Belonging in an Ancient Land', *The Hindu*, 19 March 2017, https://www.thehindu.com/society/history-and-culture/finding-treasure-in-the-neelkanth-temple-in-bundelkhand/article17530108.ece.

21. Fuhrer A. *The Monumental Antiquities and Inscriptions in the North-Western Provinces and Oude,* Superintendent of Government Press, Allahabad, 1891.

22. 'The Medieval Fort of Kalinjar and its History', Syed Ali Nadeem Rezavi, Proceedings of Indian History Congress Vol. 63, *Indian History Congress,* 2002, pp. 1233–1259.

23. Ibid.

24. Ibid.

25. Ibid.

26. Vijay Kumar and Alok Ranjan. 'Inscriptions of the Kalinjar

Fort, Kalinjar District Banda Uttar Pradesh', *Indian Journal of Archaeology*, April 2021, pp. 613–1280.

27. Ibid.

28. British Library Online Gallery, http://www.bl.ukonlinegallery/onlineex/apac/other/019wdz000000775 u00000000.html

29. British Library Online Gallery, http://www.bl.ukonlinegallery/onlineex/apac/photocoll/b/largeimage63942.html

30. British Library Online Gallery, http://www.bl.ukonlinegallery/onlineex/apac/photocoll/t/019pho000430s38 u00011000.html

31. British Library Online Gallery, http://www.bl.ukonlinegallery/onlineex/apac/photocoll/m/019pho0000002s6   u00016000.html

32. Martin, Montgomery. *The History, Antiquities, Topography and Statistics of Eastern India*, W. H. Allen, 1838.

33. Kuraishi, M.H. *List of Ancient Monuments Protected under Act VII of 1904 in the Province of Bihar and Orissa*, Government of India, Central Publication Branch, Calcutta, 1931.

34. Ibid.

35. Asher, Catherine. 'The Architecture of Raja Man Singh: A Study of Sub-Imperial Patronage', *The Powers of Art: Patronage in Indian Culture* edited by Barbara Stoler Miller, Oxford University Press, 1992.

36. Ibid.

37. Kuraishi, M. H. *List of Ancient Monuments Protected under Act VII of 1904 in the Province of Bihar and Orissa*, Government of India, Central Publication Branch, Calcutta, 1931.

38. British Library Online Gallery, http://www.bl.ukonlinegallery/onlineex/apac/photocoll/t/019pho000001003 u00474000.html.

39. Image 1–10, British Library Online Gallery, http://explore.bl.uk/primo_library/libweb/action/search. do?fn=search&ct

=search&initialSearch=true&mode=Basic&tab=website_tab
&indx=1&dum=true&srt=rank&vid=BLVU1&frbg=&tb=t&
vl%28freeText0%29=rohtasgarh&scp.scps=scope%3A%28BL
WEBSITE%29&vl%282084770706UI0%29=any&vl%2820847
70706UI0%29=title&vl%282084770706UI0%29=any

40. British Library Online Gallery, http://www.bl.uk/
   onlinegallery/onlineex/apac/other/019wdz000000200u
   00000000.html.

41. Ibid.

42. Blunt, E.A.H. *List of Inscriptions on Christian Tombs and Tablets
   of Historical Interest in the United Provinces of Agra and Oudh*,
   W. C. Abel, Government Press, United Provinces, 1911.

43. Ibid.

44. Ibid.

45. Growse, F.S. *Mathura: A District Memoir,* British Library;
   Historical Prints Editions, 2011.

46. Fanny Parkes. *Begum, Thugs and White Mughals* edited by
   William Dalrymple, Eland Publishing Ltd, 2002.

47. Abbas, Masooma. 'Ornamental Jālīs of the Mughals and Their
   Precursors', *International Journal of Humanities and Social
   Science*, Vol. 6, No. 3, March 2016, pp. 135–147.

48. Nath, Ram. *History of Mughal Architecture, Vol. I,* Abhinav
   Publications, 1982.

49. Digby, Simon. 'Sufi Diaspora, Expansion and Consolidation in
   14th Century', *Sufism and Bhakti Movement* edited by Hamid
   Hussain, Manak Publications Pvt. Ltd, 2007.

50. Eaton, Richard M. *India in the Persianate Age: 1000–1765,*
   Penguin Random House, 2020.

51. Pandey, Anjali. 'Bawdi: The Eloquent Example of Hydrolic
   Engineering and Ornamental Architecture', *International
   Journal of Research–Granthaalayah*, Vol. 4, No. 1, January 2016,

pp. 217–222, https://doi.org/10. 29121/granthaalayah. v4. i1. 2016. 2867.

52. Livingston, Morna. *Steps to Water: The Ancient Stepwells of India*, Princeton Architectural Press, 2002.

53. Ibid.

54. Ibid.

55. Gabbay, Alyssa. *Islamic Tolerance: Amir Khusraw and Pluralism*, Routledge; First Edition, 2010.

56. Minhaj-i-Siraj. *Tabaqat-i-Nasiri*, translated from Persian by Major H.G. Raverty, Gilbert & Rivington, 1881.

57. Ibid.

58. Isami and Agha Mahdi Hussain. *Futuhu's Salatin: Or, Shah Namah-i Hind of Isami Translation and Commentary*, Asia Publishing House, 1967.

59. Mohammed Habib and Khaliq Ahmad Nizami. *A Comprehensive History of India*, People's Publishing Press, 1992.

60. Eraly, Abraham. *The Age of Wrath: A History of the Delhi Sultanate*, Penguin, 2015.

61. Minhaj-i-Siraj. *Tabaqat-i-Nasiri*, translated from Persian by Major H.G. Raverty, Gilbert & Rivington, 1881.

62. Ibid.

63. Isami and Agha Mahdi Hussain. *Futuhu's Salatin: Or, Shah Namah-i Hind of Isami Translation and Commentary Volume 2*, Asia Publishing House, 1967.

64. Ibid.

65. *The Rehla of Ibn Batuta*, translated by S. Mehdi Hasan, Oriental Institute, Baroda, 1976.

66. Mohammed Habib and Khaliq Ahmad Nizami, *A Comprehensive History of India*, People's Publishing Press, 1992.

67. Minhaj-i-Siraj. *Tabaqat-i-Nasiri*, translated from Persian by Major H.G. Raverty, Gilbert & Rivington, 1881.

68. Elliot, H.M. *The History of India: As Told by Its Own Historians, The Muhammadan Period,* Trubner and Co., 1871.

69. *The Rehla of Ibn Batuta,* translated by S. Mahdi Hasan, Oriental Institute, Baroda, 1976.

70. Khan, Syed Ahmad. *Asar–us–Sanadid,* Tulika Books; Translation Edition, 2018.

71. Brown, Percy. *Indian Architecture (Buddhist and Hindu Period),* D. B. Taraporevala & Sons Pvt. Ltd, 1956.

72. British Library Online Gallery, http://www. bl. uk/ onlinegallery/onlineex/apac/photocoll/f/019pho000001003u 00676000. html

73. British Library Online Gallery, http://www. bl. uk/ onlinegallery/onlineex/apac/photocoll/c/019pho000001003u 00678000. html

74. Brown, Percy. *Indian Architecture (Buddhist and Hindu Period),* D.B. Taraporevala & Sons Pvt. Ltd, 1956.

75. Cunningham, Alexander. *Report of Tours in the Gangetic Provinces from Badaon to Bihar, 1875–76 and 1877–78,* Office of the Superintendent of Government Printing, 1880.

76. Zaheer, Muhammad. *The Temple of Bhītargāo,* Agam Kala Prakashan, 1980.

77. Ibid.

78. Kuraishi, M.H. *List of Ancient Monuments Protected under Act VII of 1904 in the Province of Bihar and Orissa,* Government of India, Central Publication Branch, Calcutta, 1931.

79. Ibid.

80. Ibid.

81. Falk, Harry, 'The Diverse Degrees of Authenticity of Aśokan Texts', *Ashoka in History and Historical Memory* edited by Patrick Olivelle, Motilal Banarsidass; First Edition, 2009.

82. Ibid.

83. Cunningham, Alexander. *Four Reports Made During the Years 1862–63–64–65*, Government Central Press, 1871.

84. Hultzsch, E. *Inscriptions of Asoka, Vol. I*, Clarendon Press, 1925.

85. *The Rehla of Ibn Batuta*, translated by S. Mehdi Hasan, Oriental Institute, Baroda, 1976.

86. British Library Online Gallery, http://www.bl.uk/ onlinegallery/onlineex/apac/other/019wdz000002095u 00017000.html.

87. British Library Online Gallery, http://www.bl.uk/ onlinegallery/onlineex/apac/other/019xzz000000400u 00011000.html

88. Royal Collection Trust, https://www.bl.uk/ collection/1005025-af/the-siege-of-daulatabad-april-june-1633.

89. Qureishi, Dulari. *Fort of Daulatabad*, Bhartiya Kala Prakashan, 2004.

90. Ibid.

91. Ibid.

92. Ibid.

93. Markel, Stephen. 'Once the Capital of India: The Great Fort of Daulatabad', Vol. 25, No. 2, *Orientations*, Orientations Magazine Ltd, 1994.

94. Gandhi, Supriya. *The Emperor Who Never Was: Dara Shukoh in Mughal India*, Bellknap Press, 2020.

95. Ibid.

96. A region comprising parts of what is now northeastern Afghanistan and southeastern Tajikistan.

97. Bilgrami, Fatima Zehra. *History of the Qadiri Order in India: 16th–18th Century*, Idarah-i Adabiyat-i Delli, 2005.

98. Gandhi, Supriya. *The Emperor Who Never Was: Dara Shukoh in Mughal India*, Bellknap Press, 2020.

99. Ibid.
100. Lawrence, Walter R. *The Valley of Kashmir*, Asian Educational Services, 2005.
101. Gandhi, Supriya. *The Emperor Who Never Was: Dara Shukoh in Mughal India*, Bellknap Press, 2020.
102. Ibid.
103. Ibid.
104. Hamdani, Sameer Hakim. *The Syncretic Traditions of Islamic Religious Architecture of Kashmir (Early 14th–18th Century)*, Routledge India, 2021.
105. Lynton, Harriet Ronken. *The Days of the Beloved*, Orient BlackSwan, 2012.
106. The J. Paul Getty Museum, http://www.getty.edu/art/collection/objects/166690/willoughby-wallace-hooper-portions-of-tombs-hyderabad-english-about-1870/.
107. Brown, Percy. *Indian Architecture (Buddhist and Hindu Period)*, D.B. Taraporevala & Sons Pvt. Ltd, 1956.
108. Balasubramanium, R. *The World Heritage Complex of the Qutub*, Aryan Books International, New Delhi, 2007.
109. British Library Online Gallery, http://www.bl.uk/onlinegallery/onlineex/apac/photocoll/c/019pho000001003u01377000.html.
110. Firishta, Muhammad Qasim. *Tarikh-e Firishta*, http://persian.packhum.org/main.
111. Mohammed Habib and Khaliq Ahmad Nizami, *A Comprehensive History of India*, People's Publishing Press, 1992.
112. Catherine B. Asher and Cynthia Talbot. *India before Europe*, Cambridge University Press, 2006.
113. Brown, Percy. *Indian Architecture (Buddhist and Hindu Period)*, D.B. Taraporevala & Sons Pvt. Ltd, 1956.
114. Ibid.

115. Basheeruddin Ahmed, *Waqiat-e-Darul Hukumat e Dehli*, Urdu Academy, Delhi.

116. Kugle, Scott. *When Sun Meets Moon: Gender, Eros, and Ecstasy in Urdu Poetry (Islamic Civilization and Muslim Networks)*, University of North Carolina Press, 2016.

117. Faruqi, Shamsur Rahman, *How to Read Iqbal? Essays on Iqbal, Urdu Poetry and Literary Theory,* Iqbal Academy Pakistan, 2007.

118. This information was relayed to the author in a personal communication.

119. Rekhta, https://www.rekhta.org/poets/nazeer-akbarabadi/profile.

120. Aquil, Raziuddin, *Locating Pleasure in Indian History*, edited by Seema Bawa, Bloomsbury, 2021.

121. Ibid.

Glossary

Aahukhana	deer park
Azaan	Islamic call to prayer
Badshah ka Takht	the king's throne
Baolis	stepwells
Baradari	twelve arched pavilion
Chabutra	platform
Chajja	wide weaves
Chatri	cupola
Chhatri	cenotaph
Chillahgahs	places for the 40 day spiritual retreats
Chini	tiles
Dard	sorrow or pain
Dhrupad	a genre of Hindustani classical music
Diwan	anthology of ghazals
Ekamukha linga	linga with the face of Lord Shiva carved on one side
Faqir	mendicant
Fateha	Quranic verses recited for the forgiveness of souls of the departed.
Gor	grave

Hammam	bathhouse
Huaz	water tank
Imam	person who leads the prayers in a mosque
Iwan	hall gallery
Jaalis	perforated screens
Jannat	paradise
Jharokhas	projecting balconies
Kalpavriksha	tree of life
Khalifa	successor
Khanqah	hospice
Kharbooza	muskmelon
Kirtimukha	it means glorious face and is the name given to a fierce monster face found in temple architecture
Kolam and *Rangoli*	geometrical designs made in front of the house with dry colors
Kund	waterbody
Kundan	traditional jewellery where gemstones are set with a gold foil between the stones and its mount
Makara	crocodile
Mandap	temple porch
Mansabdari	system a hierarchy of ranks in the Mughal court, founded by Akbar
Maqbaras	masoleum
Marsiyas	elegy
Marsiyago	poets who write elegies
Mazar	grave

Mihrab	niche in wall indicating the direction of Qiblah or direction in which Muslims pray
Mimbar	pulpit
Mimbar	pulpit
Mukhlingam	linga with a face
Muqarnas	squinch
Mushairas	poetic symposiums
Nagabandhana	entwined snakes
Nur	light
Parchinkar	inlayer
Parisar	compound
Pishtaq	a rectangular frame around an arched opening
Pujari	priest
Purdah	veil
Qalams	pens
Sahen	courtyard
Sang-e-musa	hornblende
Sarovar	water reservoir/pond
Shahikhzadas	descendants
shahr ashob	lament of a city
Shikhara	steeple
Silsilah	order
Subah	province
Surah al-Nur	twenty-fourth chapter of the Quran. The word nur means light.
Surah Fatiha	the first surah of the Quran
Takhallus	pen name

Takht	throne
Takhti	slate
Tapasya sthana	a place for the practise of austere devotions
Tassawuf	mysticism
Ulema	clergy
Urs	death anniversary
Varaha	an avatar of Lord Vishnu

Photo Credits